# The Mysterious Flame

OTHER WORKS
BY COLIN MCGINN

*The Character of Mind*

*Moral Literacy*

*Minds and Bodies:*
 *Philosophers and Their Ideas*

*Ethics, Evil and Fiction*

*Mental Content*

# The Mysterious Flame

## Conscious Minds in a Material World

### Colin McGinn

BASIC
BOOKS

A Member of the Perseus Books Group

Published by Basic Books,
A Member of the Perseus Books Group

*Designed by Rachel Hegarty*

A CIP catalog record for this book is available from the Library of Congress.
ISBN 0-465-01422-4 (cloth);
ISBN-10: 0-465-01423-2   ISBN-13: 978-0-465-01423-1 (pbk.)

The separation of spirit from matter was a mystery, and the union of spirit with matter was a mystery also.

Oscar Wilde, *The Picture of Dorian Gray*

# Contents

# Preface

It is difficult to escape from your own consciousness—your perceptions, feelings, thoughts, desires. Once your consciousness vanishes, so do you. It is with you always, a perpetual humming presence. There is nothing more evident to you than your existence as a conscious being. Yet consciousness is perplexing. What *is* consciousness? Where does it come from? How is it connected to the entity we call the body? What does the activity of the brain have to do with it? Consciousness cannot be seen or touched or pulled apart or tasted, despite its intense familiarity. It is self-evident and yet deeply puzzling. There is something *special* about it.

This book is about the mystery of consciousness. My main theme is that consciousness is indeed a deep mystery, a phenomenon of nature on which we have virtually no theoretical grip. The reason for this mystery, I maintain, is that our intelligence is wrongly designed for understanding consciousness. Some aspects of nature are suited to our mode of intelligence, and science is the result; but others are not of the right form for our intelligence to get its teeth into, and then mystery is the result. As well as explaining why this is so, I investigate the bearing of this "mysterian" thesis on a range of other questions. I am concerned here, among other things, with the geography of human ignorance, with providing a map of human knowledge and its limits.

This book is intended as an accessible synthesis of work I have done on consciousness over the last decade. My thoughts developed gradually over the years, following a sudden revelation one dark night in Oxford in 1988, when I was visited with the feeling that I had finally understood why the mind-body problem is so hard. I jumped out of bed and scribbled down some notes, thinking that they would probably seem silly to me in the morning. But the next day they made still more sense to me than anything else I had ever written or read on the mind-body problem. And the subsequent years have only confirmed this original conviction—in me, if not in others. This is my opportunity to bring these thoughts together in a way that should be intelligible to people with a general interest in the mind and its place in nature. I believe that the topic is of great relevance and concern to people outside academic circles, and I want to invite them into the debate in as clear and lively a manner as I can. Consciousness is a topic in which everyone has a vested interest; it would be good to shed as much light on it as possible, even if we have to admit in the end that it is deeply mysterious. It is also a pleasure for me to relax my habitually cautious mode of academic exposition and go straight to the heart of the big issues in plain, open language. I have accordingly written the book with the absolute minimum of jargon and technicality.

I want to thank all the people who have ever discussed the topic of consciousness with me over many points of the globe. It is a struggle to think about, no doubt about it, and the more we struggle the more tightly we feel trapped in perplexity. I am grateful for all that thrashing and wriggling. More personally, I want to thank Consuelo Preti, Catherine Mortenson, Thomas Nagel, and my son Bruno. I am grateful for their individual consciousnesses.

*Colin McGinn*
New York
October 1998

# 1

## Consciousness — Still Unexplained After All These Years

### CONSCIOUSNESS DEFINED

Imagine you are in a deep, dreamless coma. Your brain is operating on its lowest setting, merely keeping your body alive—heart beating, lungs working. Your mind is completely inactive. It is all blank within. Gradually, you begin to come out of the coma, thanks to the tireless efforts of your doctors. First you experience the position and temperature of your body; you feel comfortable and warm, no aches and pains anywhere. You hear the murmuring of the doctors, human voices all around you. There is an acrid taste in your mouth and a sensation of thirst. You catch a whiff of formaldehyde in the air. You feel confused and excited, your thoughts barely coherent. You struggle to open your eyes and a flood of bright colors assails you. Your head aches slightly, under this barrage of sights, sounds, and smells. You try to speak.

You have, as we say, recovered consciousness. All those sensations and feelings, those emotions, thoughts, and perceptions, are instances of consciousness. You were unconscious, now you are conscious: your mind is up and running again. You have made it back into the world of sentience. You are an experiencing subject once more. This transition is not simply the change from sleep to wakefulness. Remember I said you were in a *dreamless* coma. If you had been dreaming, your mind would still be working while you were asleep. You would be unconscious in one sense, unaware of your surroundings, but <u>conscious in another</u>, since you would still be <u>having sensations</u>, feelings, emotions, and thoughts. Dreams are just another form of consciousness, the kind you have when you are in the strange state called sleep. You are indeed not conscious of your surroundings while you are asleep and dreaming, but your mind still plays host to the same kinds of conscious goings-on as when you are awake. You are quite unlike a mindless rock or a brain-dead accident victim. You could in principle spend a mentally rich life in a state of uninterrupted "dreaminess." There is all the difference in the world between a dreamer and someone whose mind is a complete blank. In dreams you do not cease to experience, to be a subject of consciousness.

This inclusive phenomenon of consciousness is the topic of this book: <u>the having of sensations, emotions, feelings,</u>

thoughts. <u>Consciousness is not the same as wakefulness</u>. <u>Nor is it the same as self-awareness</u>. When you woke from the coma you experienced various sensations, but whether you reflected *on* those sensations is another question. To *experience* those sensations is not the same as to *think* that you experience them, or to say that you do. We do often reflect on our own experiences and tell each other about them, but this is not the same thing as merely having them. So we should not confuse consciousness with self-consciousness. When you are at the movies, immersed in the experience of watching the action, you seldom ascend to the level of reflecting *that* you are having all those experiences. You just *have* the experiences without forming any reflective thoughts about them. Babies presumably undergo a range of conscious states, but it is doubtful that they are reflectively self-conscious: they have no notion of self at all, at least in the early stages. And many animals are in the same state: they have a conscious life, but they do not aspire to reflect on this fact. They do not, to put it another way, apply mental *concepts* to themselves. To have a conscious state is not the same thing as applying a concept *of* that conscious state to oneself, any more than to have a certain color hair is to *describe* oneself as having that color hair. Being a certain way and characterizing yourself as being that way are logically independent facts. So we are interested here in *being* conscious, not in characterizing oneself *as* conscious—in the *fact* of consciousness, if you like, not its self-ascription. Our interest is in the sensation of pain itself, for example, not in the ability to think about the fact that you are in pain when you are.

We mature humans do, however, occasionally reflect on our consciousness. In fact this book is a prolonged reflection on it. And when we reflect on it we are struck by the fact, which so gripped René Descartes, that our consciousness is among the world's great certainties.[1] I may not be certain that I am awake now and not dreaming, and I may entertain rational doubts about whether I am really sitting at a keyboard typing, but I cannot feel this kind of insecurity about whether I am currently having experiences of a certain kind. For it certainly *seems* to me that I am typing and looking at a computer screen, even if in reality I may not be. The entire world may not exist for all I know, but my experiences of it certainly do. I can be certain of the existence and nature of my conscious experiences, even though I cannot be certain of what causes them. Thus I am certain that I am conscious: beyond a shadow of a doubt my stream of consciousness is full and flowing. I just heard a loud bang and then the sound of a car alarm in the street: hearing (the conscious state) was immediately given to me, although the cause was a matter of conjecture. This means that consciousness is a *datum*, a given, something whose existence we cannot coherently dispute. It is therefore something whose explanation we cannot duck, no matter how difficult this may be. Consciousness is always with us, as long as *we* are around.

The central topic of this book is the explanation of consciousness. Suppose I had asked you to imagine waking from a coma without having a brain in your head. You would have been rightly perplexed. Having a brain is what makes it possible to have a mental life. The brain is "the seat of consciousness." But it is not merely that the mind sits *on* the brain, like a monarch on her throne, a convenient place to take the weight off her legs. It is more that the brain is what enables the mind to exist at all; it is more of a womb than a seat. The machinery of the brain allows the mind to work as it does and to have the character it does. A queen can walk away from her throne and take a stroll in her palace gardens, but the mind is not able to detach itself from the brain in this way (if you think it can, see chapter 3). Consciousness is locked to the brain, rooted in its tissues. But this raises the question of the nature of this deep and intimate link. Can the mind be fully explained by the brain? Or are they really separate entities? What kind of thing *is* a brain, that it makes consciousness possible? What is the nature of the bond that connects our conscious experience with the workings of the gray matter in our heads?

In this book I argue that the bond between the mind and the brain is a deep mystery.[2] Moreover, it is an ultimate mystery, a mystery that human intelligence will never unravel. Consciousness indubitably exists, and it is connected to the brain in some intelligible way, but the nature of this connection necessarily eludes us. The full import of this thesis will take some time to unfold. I am especially concerned to examine the *reasons* for this mystery. I am not just throwing my hands up in despair; I am interested in uncovering the deep reasons for our bafflement and examining the consequences of our constitutional ignorance. Socrates was concerned to show people that they know less than they think they do. I too am concerned with the nature and source of human not-knowing; I want to know *why* some things are so hard to know. What *is* it about consciousness that makes it so elusive to theoretical understanding? And what is it about the knowing mind that makes it founder here? For the rest of this chapter, however, I want to articulate the problem of understanding the link between the mind and the brain further and indicate why the standard traditional responses to it do not work. Then we can move on to explore the mystery in more depth.

## Conscious Meat

Consciousness is so familiar that it is hard to appreciate what an odd phenomenon it is. We tend to take our consciousness for granted and not wonder about its origins and grounds. Let us then try to step back from our consciousness and defamiliarize it. In particular, let us try to develop a sense of the oddity of the mind-brain link. We can start with an extract from a clever science fiction story by the writer Terry Bisson.[3] (The link between mind and brain can seem like pure science fiction.) It takes the form of a conversation between an alien explorer who has visited earth and his commander:

> "They're made out of meat."
>
> "Meat?" . . .
>
> "There's no doubt about it. We picked several from different parts of the planet, took them aboard our recon vessels, probed them all the way through. They're completely meat."

"That's impossible. What about the radio signals? The messages to the stars?"

"They use the radio waves to talk, but the signals don't come from them. The signals come from machines."

"So who made the machines? That's who we want to contact."

"They made the machines. That's what I'm trying to tell you. Meat made the machines."

"That's ridiculous. How can meat make a machine? You're asking me to believe in sentient meat."

"I'm not asking you, I'm telling you. These creatures are the only sentient race in the sector and they're made out of meat."

"Maybe they're like the Orfolei. You know, a carbon-based intelligence that goes through a meat stage."

"Nope. They're born meat and they die meat. We studied them for several of their lifespans, which didn't take too long. Do you have any idea of the life span of meat?"

"Spare me. Okay, maybe they're only part meat. You know, like the Weddilei. A meat head with an electron plasma brain inside."

"Nope, we thought of that, since they do have meat heads like the Weddilei. But I told you, we probed them. They're meat all the way through."

"No brain?"

"Oh, there is a brain all right. It's just that the brain is made out of meat!"

"So. . . . what does the thinking?"

"You're not understanding, are you? The brain does the thinking. The meat."

"Thinking meat! You're asking me to believe in thinking meat!"

"Yes, thinking meat! Conscious meat! Loving meat. Dreaming meat. The meat is the whole deal! Are you getting the picture?"

The point of this parable is to bring out how surprising it is that the squishy gray matter in our heads—our brain meat—can be the basis and cause of a rich mental life. From one point of view, our prized cerebral organ *is* just a hunk of meat. After all, people do sometimes eat animal brains with potatoes and peas, and there is no hint in that culinary experience of what the tasty tissue used to accomplish when it was still the animal's organ of consciousness. (Not that I've ever tasted brains; I'm a vegetarian.) If someone were to eat your brains while you were still alive and conscious—which heaven forbid!—that person would not taste the mental events that he or she was gradually consuming. The person would certainly not taste what you were tasting as you bit into a fresh pineapple. Calling the brain "meat" is a way of classifying it along with other meaty body parts, such as muscles, kidneys, and hearts. There is nothing in this classification, itself perfectly legitimate, to prepare us for the remarkable fact that brains alone make organisms into conscious beings. Your deepest feelings might turn into a masticated mouthful if your brain falls into the wrong hands.

Can it really be true that your consciousness can be eaten and digested? The alien commander's incredulity should be ours: How *is* sentient meat possible? We know that it is possible because we all have sentient brains, but what explains this bizarre and rather comical fact? It appears so improbable to the aliens I "quoted" that minds can be engineered from the kind of thing that can be bought at a butcher's shop that they have a hard time accepting it. It *ought* not to be so, and yet, miraculously, it is. How can this be? (Of course, the same enigma exists for the aliens and their own brain unit, but they are so familiar with it in their own case that they are as complacent as we are about what makes their minds possible.)

We can state the problem this way: Isn't there some kind of violation of the uniformity of nature in the fact that brains produce consciousness? Brains seem very similar to other parts of animal bodies, being basically a big collection of cells organized according to biochemical principles. Yet there is a yawning chasm between the natures of these entities, because brains produce consciousness and those other meaty organs do not, not even a little bit. This fundamental difference is not predictable from the physical similarities we observe. If we were to observe all the body parts apart from brains, we would arrive at the conclusion that body parts do not produce consciousness. But then we encounter brains and are brought up short. They violate the natural belief that collec-

tions of cells do not generate minds. This puzzle is like observing that balls roll down hills and then discovering one that
takes off into the air of its own accord. We examine this ex-
ceptional ball from every angle, but can't find anything to distinguish it from all the others. We conclude, reasonably
enough, that nature is not uniform after all. Except that this
never happens: we always find an underlying difference that
explains the different powers of the superficially similar object. (The ball has a special kind of motor in it that is hard to
detect.) But in the case of the brain, this kind of explanation
apparently does not apply: one ball of matter does have the
power to bring consciousness into existence, but it seems so
similar to all the other mindless balls of matter rolling around
in the world. Worse yet, only *some* of the states of brains are
connected to consciousness, because some brain processes
occur without any accompanying conscious process. The parts
of the brain connected to maintaining basic bodily functions
have no conscious correlate, any more than states of the liver
do. But the two kinds of brain process appear quite similar to
each other, just neurons and their interactions. How can such
similarity mask such dissimilarity? This incongruity flies in
the face of our deep-seated and highly confirmed belief in the
uniformity of nature. How can like causes produce such vastly
unlike effects? To maintain our belief in the uniformity of nature, we are forced to deny that the brain causes the mind or
to try to find new properties of the brain to distinguish it
from other all other physical objects. We cannot just note the
violation and shrug our shoulders. The aliens are operating on

this principle when they react with such incredulity to the fact of conscious meat. None of the meat *they* have ever seen has come with an inner life. How can nature tolerate such inconsistencies in the way it works?

Some people like to harp on the complexity of the brain, as if this gave a clue to its mental productivity. But sheer complexity is irrelevant: merely adding more neurons with more synaptic connections doesn't explain our problem a bit. The problem is how *any* collection of cells, no matter how large and intricately related, could generate consciousness. The trouble is that neural complexity is the wrong *kind* of thing to explain consciousness; it is merely a matter of how many cells a given cell can causally interact with. If our kidneys had as many cells as our brains, that would not make them conscious. Nor is a galaxy conscious just because it has a tremendous number of interacting parts. If complexity is to play a role in generating consciousness, then we need to be told what *kind* of complexity is involved.

Another red herring is the "hiddenness" of the brain, the fact that it is inside an opaque skull and has an invisible interior (unless you cut it open). There is no logical necessity about this. Imagine an organism whose brain is distributed over its outside, like its skin. (Insects have an *exoskeleton;* this organism has an *exocerebrum.*) We can see its brain perfectly plainly whenever we met up with it. And suppose we are all naturally equipped with brain scanners (MRIs) that enable us to see the patterns of brain activity in this skinlike brain. I think this would make us feel the puzzle of mind and brain even more acutely than we do now, because we would not be inclined to think that the brain's inner recesses somehow correspond to the private consciousness of the Other. We would gaze in wonder at this pulsating grayish skin and wonder how *that* could possibly be the foundation of a mental life. Examining an area around the organism's left toe, we would ask ourselves how on earth an experience of red could possibly arise from such inauspicious and unpromising materials. But the tissue inside your brain that corresponds to an experience of red is really just the same *kind* of tissue as could be spread out over your left foot. Bunching up my actual skin and stuffing it into my skull certainly effects no magical transformation in its mind-generating powers. The "privacy" of consciousness has nothing to do with the fact that the brain is buried out of sight.

We can also formulate the problem historically. Consciousness has not always been here. For millions of years after the Big Bang, the universe was without life or mind, just brute matter suspended in space. Eventually life evolved on this planet (and maybe on others, too), and in the fullness of time organic brains came into existence. We can think of this slow development as the cumulative reorganization of matter under the laws of physics and biology. With evolution by natural selection, a new principle entered into the ways in which matter clumped its constituents together: the fitter the clump, the more likely it was to replicate itself. Thus, matter came to exhibit a certain sort of design, the kind that results from chance mutations being honed into organisms that reproduce more effectively than their competitors. The design of organisms is undoubtedly a remarkable fact of nature, calling for a very special kind of explanation, the kind that Darwin provided. Thus the long neck of the giraffe results from the fact that earlier giraffes with longer necks than their brethren could reach to higher places for food. The genes for longer necks were passed on more frequently than genes for shorter necks because those giraffes that could eat more had a better chance of reproducing themselves. In other words, longness of neck conferred survival advantage on giraffes that had this trait, and this produced a selection pressure that favored longer necks. But the existence of consciousness cannot be explained in this way. We are not stunned by the fact that matter is *capable* of forming the elaborate designs of animal bodies: ultimately it is all just a matter of ever more complex combinations of particles. We are not amazed that a telephone can be made from matter either, although we would be amazed if its design were not explicable in terms of some organizing principle. But in the case of consciousness the Darwinian explanation does not tell us what we need to know, for the simple reason that it is unclear how matter *can* be so organized as to create a conscious being. The problem is in the raw materials. It looks as if with consciousness a new kind of reality has been injected into the universe, instead of just a recombination of the old realities. Even if minds showed no hint of design, the same old problem would exist: How can mere matter originate consciousness? How did evolution convert the water of biological tissue into the wine of consciousness?

Consciousness seems like a radical novelty in the universe, not prefigured by the after-effects of the Big Bang, so how did it contrive to spring into being from what preceded it?

This big problem manifests itself countless times a day. Every time a sentient organism comes into existence, its consciousness freshly minted, we have the same transition from insentient matter to "mindedness." Cells combine and grow during gestation until the brain is mature enough to decant experiences: At first this clump of cells is without mentality, and before you know it there is consciousness throbbing away in there. Where does it come from? What manner of secretion is this? How does mere meat turn itself into conscious awareness? Once you were just insentient cells, no more aware of anything than your liver is now. Today you are brimming with consciousness. How did you make the grade? What catapulted you into consciousness? There must be some kind of natural process behind this astonishing leap, but this process is obscure.

Consider the universe before conscious beings came along: the odds did not look good that such beings could come to exist. The world was all just physical objects and physical forces, devoid of life and mind. The universe was as mindless then as the moon is now. The raw materials for making conscious minds—matter in motion—looked singularly unpromising as the building-blocks of consciousness. Yet now there is plenty of consciousness around, and it is as certain as anything can be. Human beings have lots of it, and the other species have their fair share, too. Just think of the amount of *pain* the universe has contained by now! It appears as if the impossible has occurred. Unconscious physical particles have conspired to generate conscious minds.

If we call the original upsurge of consciousness in the universe the "Soft Shudder," then the question becomes how to get from the Big Bang to the Soft Shudder. We have a good idea how the Big Bang led to the creation of stars and galaxies, principally by the force of gravity. But we know of no comparable force that might explain how ever-expanding lumps of matter might have developed an inner conscious life. Consider the problem in the way an astronomer might. Astronomers tell many exotic tales about the way matter behaves under certain special conditions: extremes of heat and cold, extremes of gravitational pressure, extremes of explosive power. Matter is not everywhere as mundane as it appears to us on mild little planet Earth. Black holes—those concentrations of matter so fierce in their gravitational fields that nothing can escape their iron grip, not even light—are the favorite popular example.[4] This is matter at its most occult and souped up. Black holes can only be known about indirectly, by the ripples of their extreme gravity, because no light can escape their clutches to reach our telescopes. The properties of a black hole are indeed singular and striking. But compare brains: imagine coming across these peculiar concentrations of matter in the course of your astronomical explorations. Their gravitational force is minimal, but their effects on surrounding objects are even more astounding than the effects of a black hole. Brains cause technology, society, art, science, soap operas, sin. A remarkable set of effects for such a small chunk of coagulated atoms. And the brain's influence doesn't stop there. The brain also produces inside itself a whole new dimension of reality: conscious experience. Each living brain contains its own center of thought and feeling, its own experienced world. A brain is a piece of mind-matter, a subspecies of matter in general. And like a black hole, it presents problems of knowability: that inside dimension, that subjectivity, is something that can only be inferred from external effects. Certainly no light is reflected from consciousness! A brain is a celestial object with more bizarre properties than any black hole or red dwarf or infinitely dense singularity. What would our roaming alien astronomer christen it? A "gray mind-pump," a "damp soul-source," a "mentaroid?" That astronomer would certainly need a whole new taxonomic category to do it justice. She would proceed to crack a brain open to reveal the consciousness inside it, thus dispelling the mystery of its operation. But the astronomer would be bitterly disappointed: The brain is just a soup of boring old biological cells. These mentaroids are queer objects indeed! Much head-scratching (or the alien equivalent) would ensue. What does this do to the received theories of matter?

The astronomical perspective is useful in alerting us to what a peculiar object sits in our heads. The brain begins to seem like a magic box, a font of sorcery. Thomas Huxley captured this sense of miracle beautifully when he wrote in 1886: "How it is that anything so remarkable as a state of consciousness comes about as a result of irritating nervous tissue, is just as unaccountable as the appearance of the djinn when Aladdin rubbed his lamp in the story."[5] How could simply rubbing a lamp produce something like a djinn (itself a subject of consciousness)? What have brass and oil got to do with beings like djinns? In what sense could a djinn exist *inside* a lamp (some of these djinns are huge)? The whole idea sounds like nonsense when you think about it, just a fairy tale. But, equally, how can sending an electric current into a bunch of cells produce conscious experience? What do electricity and cells have to do with conscious subjectivity? How could a conscious self exist *inside* such a soggy clump? It begins to seem that we are all djinns, each magically ensconced in our own personal brain lamps, waiting to be rubbed into life. And just as Aladdin's lamp violates the uniformity of nature, because lamps do not *generally* have such djinn-generating powers, so we appear to exist by courtesy of a breach in nature's uniformity. Electrochemical reactions don't generally result in subjective experience, yet in the case of our brains they seem to. It is all very puzzling, very puzzling indeed.

I hope that you are now feeling a cramp in your intellectual parts, a sense of mystery, even awe, that you are conscious at all. You should be thinking: *Something is wrong here*. The existence of your consciousness should strike you as a paradox, a sleight of hand. Am I now about to reveal where I mischievously led you astray and guide you back to sanity? Unfortunately, the solution to the paradox is not so simple. It will take some work to find our way out of this paradox (but it will be worth it in the end). What I want to do now is outline and criticize the standard historical approaches to the problem, just to get them out of the way. We need a fresh perspective on the problem, but first we need to know why the orthodox explanations, materialism and dualism, don't work.

## MATERIALISM

Materialism says there is nothing more to the mind than the brain as currently conceived.[6] The mind is made of meat. It *is* meat, neither more nor less. A conscious state such as seeing something red is just a bunch of neurons, brain cells, doing their physical thing. Living meat, yes, complicated meat, but meat nonetheless. We might as well call materialism "meat-ism." It is the view that consciousness is just a nice name for what you can buy in a butcher's shop: a chunk of bodily tissue.

According to materialism, we are under an illusion about the nature of the mind. Just as a straight stick looks illusorily bent in water, so the mind looks illusorily different from the brain when we look at it introspectively. Introspection is a kind of distorting lens, bending the sturdy, straight brain into a wobbly mirage of phenomenology. In reality—as distinct from mere appearance—there is no more to our mind than neurons and their electrochemical antics. Once nature (or God) put neurons in our heads, there was no more work to do to give us consciousness. This is not because neural processes merely *cause* conscious processes; it's because neural processes *are* conscious processes. Nor is it merely that conscious processes are an *aspect* of neural processes; it is rather that there is nothing more to a conscious state than its neural correlate. A pain, for example, is nothing more than a firing of certain fibers in the brain. The feeling of pain simply *reduces* to such physical processes. The two are not merely correlated; they are *identical*. Admittedly, pain does not seem like that when looked at introspectively, but introspection is a source of error and illusion, and not to be trusted in revealing the true nature of consciousness. The materialist agrees that our own awareness of our pains does not represent them *as* merely neural activity, but this is dismissed as an error of perception. The true nature of pain is not apparent to our first-person awareness of pain; rather, its nature is revealed by third-person examination of what is going on in the appropriate part of the brain. The way we are aware of our minds from the inside is held to be positively misleading as to what our minds are really like. There is thus no miracle about the way the brain produces consciousness, since consciousness is just brain activity under another name. The reason we talk the way we do about the mind is simply that we don't know enough about our brains, but there are no facts about the mind that cannot be accounted for in terms of facts about the brain. The mind is the brain in disguise. The djinn *is* the lamp, despite appearances to the contrary.

This view is very hard to swallow, even to grasp. The natural response to it is that if materialism is true, then I am not conscious after all—hence the old joke that a materialist has to feign anesthesia. We are all zombies, deluded into believing we are conscious. This natural response can be converted into a simple and straightforward argument against materialism, as follows. Suppose I know everything about your brain of a neural kind: I know its anatomy, its chemical ingredients, the pattern of electrical activity in its various segments. I even know the position of every atom and its subatomic structure. I know everything that the materialist says your mind is. Do I thereby know everything about your mind? It certainly seems not. On the contrary, I know nothing about your mind. I know nothing about which conscious states you are in— whether you are morose or manic, for example—and what these states feel like to you. So knowledge of your brain does not give me knowledge of your mind. How then can the two be said to be identical?

One reply to this argument is that facts are one thing and knowledge of facts another. Perhaps I do thereby know all the facts about your mind; it is just that I know about them by using other concepts. The materialist claims that all mental facts are brain facts, not that we can *translate* concepts for mental facts into concepts for brain facts. After all, all the facts about water are facts about $H_2O$, although the words "water" and "$H_2O$" do not mean the same thing: they are not synonyms. The trouble with this reply is that there is no way to distinguish mental and physical concepts without appealing to a distinction at the level of facts. What makes the concept *pain* different from the concept *C-fiber firing* is precisely that the two concepts express distinct properties, so we cannot say that these properties are identical. The materialist is forced to introduce the idea of two different appearances of the same fact, but this notion of appearance itself depends upon there being facts of appearance that cannot be identified with brain facts. The appearance of pain cannot be reduced to C-fiber firing, just as the appearance of water cannot be reduced to $H_2O$. But appearances are what the mind consists of. So the mind cannot be reduced to the brain.

Another way to approach the problem is based on an argument of the Australian philosopher Frank Jackson.[7] It concerns a rather unusual imaginary person called Mary. Mary is born and raised in a black-and-white room; she never has any color experiences apart from these. But Mary is a talented physicist and she learns everything physical about the human brain from a black-and-white television set in her room; in time she becomes the world's leading expert on brain science. There is nothing physical about the brain that Mary doesn't know. In particular, she knows the neural correlate of every kind of conscious state. One day the door to her black-and-white room is unlocked and she is set free into the world of color. Her eyes first alight upon a red rose and she has her first ever experience of red. She is mightily impressed (and probably resentful about all those achromatic years) and says, "Well, I knew a lot before, but now I have learned something new—what an experience of red is like." And this seems to be true: she knows something now that she did not know while still in her room. She has become acquainted with a property she was ignorant of before. But if that is true, then she did *not* know everything about the mind while still in her room, despite her complete knowledge of the brain. Therefore,

complete knowledge of the brain does not add up to knowledge of the mind, and the thesis of materialism is false. Nor
can Mary protest that she merely learns a new appearance for
the same old facts, because an appearance is itself a mental
thing, and she did not grasp that appearance while still in the
room. There is something she was missing. And that something is nothing other than consciousness itself. In knowing
everything about the brain, she knew nothing about what it is
like to have conscious experiences. Her knowledge of consciousness came from her own introspective access to her
own consciousness, not from the wealth of physical knowledge she acquired while still in the room. And since she had
not experienced red before she was released into the world
of color, she did not know what this experience would be
like. All that physical knowledge did not prepare her for "red."

Another way to make the point derives from the work of
Brian Farrell, an Oxford philosopher, and Thomas Nagel, a
philosopher at New York University.[8] Bats navigate in the dark
by emitting high-pitched shrieks that rebound off objects and
return echoes into their exquisitely tuned ears. This sense,
called echo-location, is unlike any that we humans possess.
No doubt bats experience certain distinctive sensations when
they echo-locate: this is what bat phenomenology consists of.
What it is like to be a bat involves this echo-locatory phenomenology. But this phenomenology is alien to us, because we
have no such sense. Just as a man born blind does not know
what it is like to see, so we do not know what it is like to
echo-locate as bats do. We do not grasp the inner character of

bat experiences. But this ignorance on our part does not extend to knowledge of a bat's brain. A bat's brain is very like other brains, the standard-issue gaggle of neurons all hooked up together into a dense lattice. We could know all about the bat's brain as a material system, but that would not give us knowledge of what it is like to be a bat. It would not remedy our present ignorance. It would not give us complete insight into the bat's consciousness. Thus, knowledge of the brain does not amount to knowledge of the mind. In the same way, human phenomenology is not reducible to our physiology, since an alien scientist who did not share our senses would not learn our phenomenology just by delving into our brains. This is just a fancy way of saying that there is a deep logical gap between neurons and experiences, between our mental nature and our physical nature. The materialist tries to cross this gap by brute force, but the gap stubbornly remains. The reason, then, that introspection does not reveal the mind to be the brain is just that the mind is not in fact the brain. It is not that introspection is blind to the true nature of mental states. Rather, mental states are not reducible to neural states, and introspection reveals this fact.

## Dualism

Materialism is the "scientific" view of the mind. It is not the commonsense view. The commonsense view is much closer to dualism.[9] Dualism comes in different forms, but for our purposes it is best interpreted as the belief that there is no

logical relation between brain and mind. There is no possibility of reducing the mind to the brain, because they are separate realms. There are indeed empirical and contingent relations between the two—correlations between mental and
physical processes have been discovered—but there is no necessary link between consciousness and the brain. Mind and
brain run in parallel, like skis, but we cannot collapse the one
into the other. They are distinct existences. The reason we
cannot explain the mind by reference to the brain is simply
that it is not essentially dependent upon the brain. Consciousness is an extra feature of the universe, as basic as space and
time and matter themselves. This is precisely why knowledge
of the brain does not give knowledge of the mind, the same
reason that knowledge of chalk does not give knowledge of
cheese: because they are different things. There is not one
world with different descriptions, as materialism holds; the
mind and the brain are two worlds, running in tandem.

I discuss dualism in more detail in chapter 3, but for now
let us consider some of the stranger consequences of this position. It is not that dualism is mistaken in its response to the
data: consciousness certainly *seems* quite different from a mere
brain process. My hearing of a loud bang, say, presents itself
as a different *kind* of thing from electrical activity in a certain
part of my brain. And thinking about a trip to the beach does
not *feel* like the spiking of innumerable neurons in my cortex.
The problem is that dualism goes too far in accommodating
the data. It responds to the appearances by declaring the mind
quite independent of the brain. It renders the brain irrelevant

to the mind in a way that it cannot be. In trying to do justice to the appearances, it misrepresents the hard realities of the mind-brain connection.

There are two major problems with dualism, the "zombie problem" and the "ghost problem". The zombie problem is that dualism allows us to subtract the mind from the brain while leaving the brain completely intact. Consider your brain now, whirring and chugging away, and consider your present state of consciousness. Dualism says that we can coherently imagine that your brain stays the same while we "suppose" your consciousness away. The two are distinct, so you can have one without the other. The result is a zombie, a being just like you physically but having no mental life whatever. It walks and talks, sighs and groans, laughs and cries—but there is no one home. Inside it is a blank, a mere robot, devoid of sense and feeling, yet it acts just as you do, even down to the last detail. This is not one of those fumbling zombies, arms dangling, that you see in horror movies. This is your top-of-the-line zombie, a perfect replica of conscious you. Even your mother couldn't tell the difference. All we have done, says the dualist, is subtract the mental properties while leaving your physical nature perfectly intact.

This sounds coherent enough, if slightly unnerving, until we notice that the zombie possibility implies the doctrine known as *epiphenomenalism*. Epiphenomenalism is the claim that mind doesn't matter, that it makes no difference what happens in the world, that it does not cause behavior. My zombie twin behaves just like me but has no mind at all. How then can it be that *my* mind affects my behavior? My mind must be like a lazy halo floating over my brain, unable to influence the course of events. This problem is particularly acute when we consider what I say about my own mind. Suppose I say the words "I am having an experience of red" just when I am in fact experiencing red. It is overwhelmingly natural to suppose that it is my experience of red that explains my saying those words: I am simply reporting my current experience. I say what I do *because* of what I experience. But my zombie twin says the same words, since he is a physical duplicate of me, and yet he *has* no experience of red, no experience at all. So in *his* case the explanation of his saying those words is not that he is having an experience of red. Rather, the explanation relies on the physical events in his brain and the way they trigger his speech mechanisms. But then surely my words must have the *same* explanation, because the same effects must have the same explanation, and certainly just those physical events were going on in me. But this means that my experience played no role in causing my words after all. It was causally redundant, epiphenomenal. So we get the perplexing—and ultimately unsatisfying—result that my experiencing red has nothing to do with my saying that I experience red. Dualism makes my mind into an idle spectator of what happens to my body. The only way to restore efficacy to the mind is to strengthen its ties to the brain, so that it is not possible to peel the mind off the brain and leave the brain as it was. The mind must be more bound up with the brain than dualism allows. In particular, the way the mind causes behavior must somehow recruit the brain, or else it cannot cause behavior.

The ghost problem is the converse to the zombie problem. If the mind is separate from the body, then not only can the brain exist without the mind but the mind can exist without the brain. Disembodiment becomes a real possibility, not just a funny fantasy. Some people may welcome this result, since it fits in nicely with religious doctrines (discussed in chapter 3). But others of a more scientific bent will find this a hard result to swallow. For now let me make the point that a disembodied mind is difficult to tie down to the physical world. How could such a mind be located anywhere without a body to anchor it? How can it have effects in the physical world? How could we manage to pick out and describe one disembodied mind rather than another? We can hardly *point* to a disembodied mind. When we picture a ghost to ourselves we indulge in a contradictory mishmash of the immaterial and the corporeal, an entity that can be seen but not touched, that can walk through walls yet can pick things up, that produces sounds from no vocal apparatus, that has a surface but no interior organs. When you reflect on ghosts they make no sense, not as potentially real presences in the world. It is the same with ghostly disembodied minds. We think we can imagine detaching ourselves from our bodies and floating away in space to a happier place. But this idea is fraught with conceptual difficulties. Why do we have complex brains at all if they are so dispensable in the functioning of our minds? Why does brain damage obliterate mental faculties if minds do not owe their existence to brains? Why were there not minds floating about before brains ever evolved? Why are all mental changes actually accompanied by brain changes? The fact is that minds have their deep roots in brains. They are not just temporary residents of brains, like wandering nomads in the desert. Deracinate them and they lose their handle on reality. Minds don't merely occupy brains, they are somehow constituted by brains. That is why the minds of different species vary, why minds develop in concert with brains, why the health of your brain makes all the difference to the life of your mind. Minds and brains are not ships that pass in the night; the brain is the very lifeblood of the mind.

The problem with materialism is that it tries to construct the mind out of properties that refuse to add up to mentality. It assumes that if you put enough pieces of neural chalk together you will eventually get some conscious cheese. The trouble with dualism is that it cuts the mind off too radically from the brain. It assumes that the mind can go about its business without the machinery of the brain to assist it. Is there any other position to consider? The purpose of this book is to develop and defend another position. Let me now state briefly and programmatically the position I am proposing. My thesis is that consciousness depends upon an unknowable natural property of the brain. What this means is that I am not going to try to reduce consciousness to those mundane known properties of neurons that materialists hope to get by with. But neither am I going to conceive of consciousness as something apart from the brain, something with no further analysis or explanation. <u>Consciousness is rooted in the brain</u> <u>via *some* natural property of brain tissue</u>, but it is not explicable in terms of electrochemical processes of the familiar kind. I shall argue that it is the very unknowability of this property that generates all our perplexities. The materialists are right to think that it is *some* property of the brain that is responsible for consciousness, but they are wrong in the *kind* of brain property they select. The dualists are right to doubt that the brain as currently conceived can explain the mind, but they are wrong to infer that *no* brain property can do the job. Both views overestimate our knowledge of mind and brain, presupposing that our current conceptions are rich enough to capture the essence of the mind-brain link. I maintain that we need a qualitative leap in our understanding of mind and brain, but I also hold that this is not a leap our intellectual legs can take. Having examined the weaknesses of the standard approaches, we should now feel ready to explore this possibility. What I have tried to do in this chapter is articulate the nature of the problem of consciousness and bring out how very difficult it is to resolve. The problem is sharp and real, profound and inescapable, and the standard ways of responding to it are non-starters, stabs in the dark with a blunt knife. If it were not for the fact that these approaches have dominated the discussion for the last two thousand years, I would suggest putting them out of mind altogether. Wipe the mental slate clean. We need another perspective entirely. The rest of this book is devoted to developing such a perspective.

# 2

# Natural Mysteries and Biased Minds

## KNOWLEDGE AND IGNORANCE

To understand why the problem of consciousness is so baffling, we need to step back and examine the nature of human knowledge. After all, in trying to solve the mind-body problem we are seeking a certain item of knowledge, and the question must arise about what kind of knowledge this would be and whether we can actually acquire it. My overall thesis is that our troubles here stem from constitutional limits on our powers of understanding; so we should begin with a general examination of human knowledge, its scope, and its limits. Then we can return to the specific issue of understanding the relationship between the mind and the brain.

Thought is clearly not the same thing as reality. A thought is something that goes through a person's mind, while reality in general does not (although thoughts are also one part of reality). A thought is a means of representing reality, an attempt to pin reality down. If I have the thought "It is snowing outside," my mind represents the world as currently snowy, and if it is actually snowy then my thought is true. But of course snow itself is not the same thing as a thought about snow: snow is cold but thoughts about it are not. A thought, moreover, is made up of concepts, which are strung together to represent a state of affairs. Which states of affairs your mind can represent depends upon which concepts your mind has at its disposal. If I didn't have the concept *snow*, then I would not be able to represent the world as snowy. There, on the one hand, is the world with all its objects and properties, existing independently of us; here, on the other hand, is thought about the world, consisting of concepts that may or may not cover everything there is in the world. It is because of this fundamental divide between thought and reality that human knowledge is problematic. Knowledge is the attempt by the mind to keep track of reality, to embrace it in thought. It is the mind trying to get beyond itself. This is an enterprise fraught with difficulties and pitfalls, because reality does not always yield up its secrets so easily, and the mind does not always function optimally. Knowledge is a kind of marriage of mind and world, and like all marriages it has its failures and frustrations, its disharmonies and misalignments. Knowledge is not something to be taken for granted, by any means.

Not every fact about the world is knowable. There are facts that no one can know. How do I know this? Don't I need to know the facts before I can know whether or not they are knowable? Actually, no—I do know there are certain facts that I cannot know, and so do you. For example, there was once a definite number of dinosaurs in the world, quite a large number. Call that number N. Do I know what number N is? Certainly not: I have no idea how many dinosaurs there were. Neither does anyone else. And neither could anyone else. We will never be able to establish from the fossil record or from other sources of evidence exactly how many dinosaurs roamed the earth. Similarly for the question of how many ants there were in Africa in the year 1620. Our knowledge of the past is partial and patchy, and typically confined to generalities. Nor is this ignorance remediable, because the past does not leave enough traces of itself to answer every question about what it contained. The future is no different. There are obviously many things about the future I do not know and never will know in my lifetime. And there surely are some truths about the future that no human being will ever know, given that the human race will eventually become extinct when the sun goes dead on us. The future is a vast ocean of human ignorance.

The infinite is a rich source of human not-knowing. If space and time are infinite, then their very structure imposes strict limits on our knowledge of them. No finite mind could encompass all of space and time. No speed of space travel could ever exhaust infinite space, and even time-travel could never take us to every time, given that time is infinite in both directions. We are finite beings poised at one specific location in space and time, like beads on an unending string, with both dimensions streaming away from us into infinity. We know something about this infinite world, but surely not very much.

Since the time of the ancient Greeks skeptics have stressed our ignorance.[1] How do we really know that we are not dreaming, that other people have minds, that the future will resemble the past? How do we really know anything that exists beyond our current state of consciousness? <u>Our so-called knowledge is thoroughly based on inference, but inference is fallible.</u> A favorite skeptical example is the brain in a vat: How do you know that your brain has not been removed from your head and placed in a vat of nutrients by unscrupulous superscientists who are simulating the environment by means of electrodes implanted in your brain? Your reason for believing you are inhabiting the ordinary world is that your experience has a certain consistent pattern, but that pattern could in principle be produced artificially, simply by mimicking the sensory inputs you receive. It might all be one giant hallucination. Following such speculation, we start to wonder how knowledge is possible at all. As I remarked in the previous chapter, only one's own current state of consciousness seems immune to such doubts. Knowledge seems harder to acquire than we naively suppose. Ignorance is the human lot.

The fragility of human knowledge also shows up in cases where it seems to be just cosmic luck that we have the kind of evidence that we do have for how things are. Take astronomy: for centuries the inherent difficulty of knowing about such distant objects as stars and galaxies prevented astronomers from advancing very far—we couldn't just pack a bag and take a trip to the stars in hopes of discovering their secrets. We have to make painstaking observations from tiny planet Earth, stuck in one corner of a huge galaxy, noting the orbits of the observable bodies in nearby space. Only in this century has the science of astronomy been able to make giant leaps forward, thanks to a single central fact: that light from the stars reaches planet Earth and our telescopes and measuring devices. But that is a highly contingent fact. Imagine a universe in which the vast majority of stars emitted no light at all, being cold lumps rather than fiery furnaces. In that universe our main means of knowing about the stars would not exist, and so we would remain in ignorance of their properties and distance from us. Or suppose that Earth were covered in a thick mantle of cloud, which let in just enough light and heat from the sun to sustain life but occluded the rest of the universe. That would put a stop to any serious study of the stars. My point is that human knowledge depends upon the right kind of mediation between world and mind. The world has to be so arranged that the mind *can* take in its properties. We have to be in the right relation to the facts we want to know about if we are to succeed in knowing those facts. And there is never any guarantee that the right knowledge-conferring relationship exists. Knowledge is never a foregone conclusion.

There are two basic viewpoints about human knowledge. One contends that we exist in a natural state of ignorance, with local and unreliable incursions of knowledge to relieve the oceans of uncertainty. From this viewpoint we should count ourselves lucky to know what we do know. The other

approach sees us as natural knowers, beings whose birthright
is eventual omniscience. From this perspective everything
will finally yield to the inquiring mind. We have the right
tools in our heads to grasp every truth about the world, given
enough time and effort. This second viewpoint, or ideology,
pervades the conception of ourselves that is the legacy of the
scientific revolution begun in the seventeenth century. It is
seldom explicitly articulated, but it governs the way we tend
to think about the powers of the human mind today. It is an
intelligible response to the enormous strides made in the
physical sciences, but I believe that it overreaches in ways that
the first viewpoint serves to correct. For the question is
whether the concepts and methods that have proved so star-
tlingly successful in one domain—the workings of the physical world—can be carried over with the same degree of success to the world of the mind. Will these methods work in
enabling us to understand the nature of consciousness? We
certainly cannot infer that *since* we understand the physical
world so well it is only a matter of time until we understand
consciousness, because consciousness is so different from
what has so far yielded to our understanding. That would be
like inferring that steel can be molded with bare hands because plasticine can be. The only way to justify such an inference would be to show that consciousness is just physical, but
that we saw not to be so in the previous chapter. So the question of the knowability of the place of consciousness in the
natural world remains moot. We may or may not be able to
arrive at a proper understanding of its deep workings.

## The Structure of Intelligence

To pursue this question further we need to interrogate human intelligence: What kind of thing is intelligence, and what might its limitations stem from? It used to be thought that the mind is a blank slate, a *tabula rasa*: the mind begins life with nothing inscribed upon it and it acquires its contents and capacities purely as a result of experience or learning. The idea was that intelligence is basically memory storage, a sort of mental warehouse. It is not divided up into separate, specialized faculties, but is rather a kind of all-purpose, problem-solving device. Any limits it has have to do only with its informational capacity. (This picture was encouraged by the equating of intelligence with something called IQ, a quantity held to measure a person's "general intelligence".) The reason a human mind differs from that of a monkey or a cat is just that we have a greater storage capacity than they do and the course of our experience has been different. In principle, you could put a human brain into a monkey's environment and it would come out with a monkey's mind. Intelligence is indefinitely plastic, environmentally shaped, and essentially homogeneous.

However, this view has now been roundly rejected. The view of cognitive functioning now widely accepted stresses three features of intelligence: innateness, modularity, and adaptation.[2] We are not concerned here with individual differences in intelligence between members of a given species—which, for understandable reasons, tends to be what interests most of us. We are concerned rather with the general character of the mind of a given species. Individuals differ in all sorts of ways in their bodily anatomy, but there is also a general type of anatomy enjoyed by a given species—human, monkey, cat, or whatever. In the case of the body it is easy to see that the body is made up of a collection of organs that are innately specified and designed to perform a specific function. We do not *learn* to have arms and legs and kidneys; we have these organs as a result of our species-specific genetic endowment. And each bodily organ has its assigned function, what it is designed by nature to do. The specialization of each organ is known as modularity: the idea that the body is a collection of differenti- ated units with specific functions and designs. So in the case of the body no one would think that we are blank slates whose bodies are shaped by experience from some initial formless blob. Our bodies are innately fixed, modular in structure, and exhibit a functional division of labor.

It is just this conception that we now apply to the mind as well. Consider our capacities for speech and sight. Distinct parts of the brain are dedicated to these two faculties, and they clearly differ in their structure and function. The visual faculty is designed to take in information about objects in the organism's environment, while the language faculty has the job of symbolically transmitting thoughts from one organism to another (among other things). The visual faculty represents edges, depth, color, and motion; the language faculty repre- sents the syntax and meaning of sentences. These are distinct mental modules with innate bases and specific job descrip- tions. They both possess a rich internal structure that permits them to function as they do. This internal structure is selective: the faculties will not work if the environment of the organism does not fit the assumptions built into each module. The visual system is adapted to the kind of physical world in which it evolved, in which certain patterns of light on the retina are correlated with certain ways objects exist in the world beyond. If the laws of optics were to change suddenly, then the visual system would start to misrepresent the environment systematically. Similarly, if you place a human child in a linguistic environment that does not conform to the rules of human grammar, then its language module will be unable to extract the right rules from the acoustic flux. The innate language module is targeted toward the grammar of human languages; place the child in a Martian linguistic environment, where the rules of grammar are very different, and the child will fail to acquire Martian language. To be a master of a particular trade is to have a fixed set of specific capacities that do not transfer to other trades. <u>Intelligence is always intelligence</u> *at* or *for* <u>something.</u>

It is easy to appreciate this point if we compare the minds of different species. Ants are remarkably intelligent at cooperating in joint ventures of foraging and nest building, but their algebra and French are not of a high standard. Dogs and cats have impressive olfactory intelligence—they can sniff out a mouse far better than you or I—but they are less adept when it comes to table manners. Many animals, especially birds, have highly acute motion perception compared to humans, but their foveal vision—the kind we use when focusing on something right in front of us—is pretty poor. We are innately equipped to speak, but no other animal has this faculty. The list goes on. The plain fact is that the different brains of different species are genetically programmed to excel in certain tasks and not to be concerned about others, and this division of expertise corresponds closely to the biological needs of the organism. The minds of different species are as complex and specialized as their bodies, just as we would expect. There is no meaningful general notion of intelligence that enables us to declare one species "more intelligent" than another, if by intelligence we mean the ability to fulfill the goals of the organism. If sheer survival power is made the measure of intelligence, then ants and cockroaches and even viruses come out ahead of us. You don't need to be a rocket scientist to make it through the evolutionary night.

The prevailing view in cognitive psychology today is that the human mind consists of separate faculties, each dedicated to certain cognitive tasks: linguistic, social, practical, theoretical, abstract, spatial, and emotional. The mind is thus as highly structured as the body. Sometimes a person may be lacking in one or more of these modules. Autistic children are unable to interact with other people normally—their module for social intelligence is functionally impaired in some way. Dyslexics have a genetic disability when it comes to recognizing letters and so experience reading difficulties. Prosopagnosics are unable to recognize faces, even of those nearest and dearest to them, although their vision is otherwise unimpaired. Such people are not in any general sense unintelligent;

they are simply lacking in one highly specific component of what we think of as normal human intelligence. Evolution has equipped us with a large number of these modules, each with its own job to do. Thus we have certain biases built into our mental architecture, certain things we are adapted for as against others.

## How Is Science Possible?

The mind is an evolved box of contrivances, adapted for solving problems that are relevant to the organism's needs. How then is science possible—and art, and philosophy, and all the rest of what we call "culture?" The answer must be that these are all by-products of capacities that exist in us for other more pragmatic reasons. Why are some humans capable of ballet dancing? Not, surely, because ballet dancing is of any biological utility, but because it is an offshoot of motor capacities that are biologically useful: catching, fleeing, maneuvering in tight corners. The musculature and motor coordination that we have because of biological imperatives can be diverted into other uses—in this case the pursuit of the art of dancing. And something similar must be true of the higher intellectual pursuits, too. We can understand science and mathematics and philosophy by virtue of the kind of intelligence that results from frontal lobes like ours, which evolved for specific biological reasons (although it is a matter of speculation what these reasons were). Evolved traits always have their by-products and fall-out, and human intelligence is no exception to this rule. What we are pleased to call "civilization" is basically biological overspill, etiologically speaking.

But there are bound to be limitations that result from the initial function of the capacities in question. The ballet dancer can jump abnormally high, but not over twenty feet. He is flexible, but not arbitrarily so. The scientist is a skilled thinker, but she cannot remember more than her finite memory capacity allows, and she cannot think a million thoughts a second. Every mental faculty has limits to its achievements and acuity, and necessarily so. If it were not so, we would be supernatural beings, like God, who suffers no such bounds or biases. But we are natural beings, descended from apes, living in a natural world, and our capacities are as finite as can be. We can, it is true, do more with our minds than apes can, but that does not mean that we somehow magically escape the constraints of biology. We are animals all the way down, or up, not angels.

It is an odd fact of evolution that we are the only species on Earth capable of creating science and philosophy. There easily could have been another species with some scientific talent, say that of the average human ten-year-old, but not as much as adult humans have; or one that is better than us at physics but worse at biology; or one that is better than us at everything. Greater or lesser fluency in spatial reasoning could produce such discrepancies of scientific intelligence, as could varying mathematical capacities. The television show *Star Trek* teems with aliens whose cognitive capacities exceed ours in various respects, with some that are markedly inferior to us—and they have the skull shapes to prove it. If there were such creatures all around us, I think we would be more willing to concede that human scientific intelligence might be limited in certain respects. We might even concede that we are subject to certain blindspots and oversights in theoretical matters. We have a human tendency to admit limitation only when someone else can visibly out-do us.

## COGNITIVE CLOSURE

Let us imagine two possible kinds of mind that would exhibit obvious limitations, so that we can then ask whether we might be in the same position with respect to the problem of consciousness. David Hume, the seventeenth-century empiricist philosopher, held that concepts are formed in the mind by a procedure of copying the impressions of sense that the subject receives from the environment.[3] An impression of red comes in through the eyes and the mind takes a copy of it, fainter in vividness, and stores it in memory, like a kind of sensory memo. Thinking is the activation and deployment of these stored copies. Hence Hume's famous dictum that there is "nothing in the mind which was not previously in the senses." The mind cannot contain a concept that was not initially based on what the senses reveal about the world. As Hume recognized, this places severe limits on the representational powers of the mind: basically, if you can't see it you can't think about it either. He thus held, consistently enough, that we have no genuine concepts of identity through time for material objects, or of selves, or of causal necessity, because we do not have sensory impressions of any of these things. The Humean theory of the human mind is immensely implausible, but we can certainly *imagine* a mind that works by Humean principles. Maybe some animal minds are rather like this, limited in their scope to what the animal can perceive. All such animals have in their heads by way of concept-forming machinery is a sensory photocopier. Such a mind would clearly be unable to grasp scientific theories. The notion of a law of nature would be unavailable to it, as would all those unobservable entities that are the glory of science as we know it. The atomic conception of matter would be out of the question for such a mind, not to mention quantum theory and relativity theory. These theories would be, as I like to say, *cognitively closed* to a Humean mind. It is pretty clear that such theories are cognitively closed to the minds of dogs and monkeys, but in the case of the Humean mind we can see exactly why the closure operates so definitively: there is no sensory original from which the needed concepts can be derived by copying. You can't *see* an atom.

Or consider a mind whose sensory faculties are far more limited than ours. This mind can sense only sounds or smells, let us say. Clearly the spatial representations of the world accessible to such a mind would be highly truncated. Without sight and touch, the spatial senses *par excellence*, our spatial awareness of the world would be severely impoverished. And this would have ramifications for the general conception of the spatial world available to a mind with such meager sensory inputs. It is doubtful that the notion of a spatial manifold containing objects of certain shapes and sizes, and occupying positions relative to one another, could be constructed on this limited basis. And if this general notion could not be formed, then the theoretical understanding of the world that depends upon it could not formed either. Again, science would be impossible for a mind so constrained.

Now the question is whether our minds are, from a superior conceptual standpoint, similarly impoverished with respect to certain domains of reality, specifically our own consciousness. Surely this cannot be ruled out *a priori*: it is the purest dogmatism to believe that the human mind, at this particular stage of evolutionary history, has reached the pinnacle of cognitive capacity. On the contrary, there are all sorts of natural limitations to human intelligence, as we are all painfully aware. So if we encounter an area of inquiry in which we seem systematically unable to make any real progress, we should at least consider the possibility that we are running up against our cognitive limits. Our understanding surely *has* bounds, just as a matter of general principle, so we should be alert to signs in our cognitive life that such bounds are making themselves felt. The enemy may lie within the gates.

I maintain that the perennial puzzlement surrounding consciousness and its relation to the body is an indication that we are on the edge of what we can make comprehensible to ourselves. Human intelligence, as I have stressed, is an evolutionary contrivance, designed with purposes far removed from the solution of profound philosophical problems, and it is not

terribly surprising if it lacks the tools to crack every problem. There is no inevitability about the existence of intelligence as we have it anyway; most animals get by perfectly well
without it. And it is not inevitable that we will be able to solve
the problems of mind that so perplex us by using this intelligence. Human intelligence is but a blip on the evolutionary
time-line, and may not be destined to persist into the evolutionary future. There is no product warranty inscribed on our
brains reading, "This device is guaranteed to solve any problem it can formulate. If not completely satisfied, please return to Philosophical Products Inc. for a sincere apology and
your money back." With this general point in mind, then, let
us consider where exactly our cognitive faculties might be
letting us down in trying to solve the mind-body problem.

## FUGITIVE CONCEPTS

How do we form our concepts of consciousness and the
brain? What determines the way we think about these two
things? Despite the deep connection between mind and brain,
there is a sharp distinction in the faculties through which we
apprehend them. I form my concepts of consciousness
through examining my own inner conscious states, that is,
through acts of self-awareness. What is pain? Pain is that feeling I get when I stub my toe or cut my finger, the feeling that
I experience "from the inside." I form my concepts of the
brain, on the other hand, by perceptual means. I have actually
to *look* at the brain, touch it, smell it—make observations of

it. I use my outer senses to acquaint myself with the properties of brains. To gross observation, a brain looks like a large
gray walnut. At a more microscopic level it consists of an
elaborate network of crisscrossing fibers, with little bulbs and
protrusions. We learn about the brain the way we learn about
other material objects, by perception augmented with instruments that enhance perception (notably the microscope).

These two points are entirely obvious: we are aware of consciousness inwardly, while we are aware of the brain out-
wardly. But now note this: introspection cannot teach you a
thing about the brain as a physical object, even though consciousness is a property of the brain, and outer perception
cannot give you any access to consciousness, even though
consciousness is rooted in the observable brain. There must
be an underlying unity in the mind-brain link, but there is an
irreducible duality in the faculties through which we come to
know about mind and brain. You can look into your mind until
you burst, and you will not discover neurons and synapses and
all the rest; and you can stare at someone's brain from dawn
till dusk and you will not perceive the consciousness that is so
apparent to the person whose brain you are so rudely eye-
balling. You may indeed perceive the physical *correlates* of a
conscious state, as with a PET scan of what is going on inside
the brain of someone whose consciousness is in a particular
kind of state. The temperature and electrical activity of different brain locations may reveal something about what state of
consciousness the person is undergoing. But this is not the
same as perceiving the state of consciousness *itself,* what that

state is like for the person undergoing it. What we see in the
PET scan is nothing like what it feels like for the person
whose brain we are scanning. And we would have no reason,
based upon the PET scan alone, to attribute consciousness to
the brain we are observing; for this we require that the person in question corroborate an attribution of conscious state.
Even hi-tech instruments like PET scans only give us the
physical basis of consciousness, not consciousness as it exists
for the person whose consciousness it is. Yet somehow the
brain and consciousness are bound together into an intelligible whole. It *ought* to be the case that we have some kind of
faculty that can catch the mind and brain in their natural state
of union, but we have to make do with what we have—and
this does not disclose the unity that must exist in reality. It is
as if we are forced to apprehend the mind from one angle, the
one accessible to introspection, while we are confined to another angle when we apprehend the brain, the one accessible
to perception. It is a bit like having to view an elephant either
from the tail end or the trunk end and never being allowed to
take in the whole elephant. You might well come to think that
the idea of a unitary elephant is elusive at best, bogus at
worst. One wants to say, "If only we could examine the brain
introspectively and perceive consciousness, *then* we would be
on the track of the nature of the connection." It is as if the faculties we must employ are wrongly targeted to give us the information we need.

We can make this point a bit more precisely. There is some
property of the brain, let's call it C*, that explains how con-

sciousness emerges from neural tissue. We do not know what C* is, but we know it has to be there. When a hunk of matter has C*, it necessarily has consciousness. How are we to identify this property? What faculty shall we use? Introspection will not do the job, because it is confined to the surface of consciousness. It tells you what is currently in your consciousness, not how your consciousness comes to exist in the first place. C* is too close to the brain to be identifiable by inwardly inspecting and noting your state of consciousness. In other words, you are not going to solve the mind-body problem simply by paying attention to what you are now experiencing, because that experience contains no hint of its material substrate in the brain. The introspective analysis of consciousness can be interesting and useful, but it is not going to reveal the means by which consciousness is embodied in matter. Introspection does not present consciousness *as* an aspect of the physical brain.

Far more promising, at least to the scientifically minded, is to investigate the brain directly. If we look hard enough inside the crevices of the cortex, we will eventually come across the property C*. It may not be visible right there in the cerebral convolutions, an especially radiant streak of white tissue, emitting an eerie sparkle under the microscope, but it is some more subtle aspect of brain functioning, possibly a fancy orchestration of electrical impulses from all segments of the cerebral hemispheres. But this is pure fantasy. The key point here is that just as consciousness itself is not, as a matter of principle, visible in the brain, so C*—which constitutes the very essence of consciousness—is not visible either. That is not too surprising in itself, because there is no *a priori* reason to suppose that every theoretically interesting property of the world is perceptible (think of quantum theory). But in those other cases we at least have a natural way to project our understanding beyond the perceptual appearances: we ask what we would need to explain what we do observe and then postulate the necessary explanatory properties. This is how we form the idea of an invisible world of elementary particles whose properties explain the behavior of gross perceptible matter. Can we use this strategy to get to C*?

The problem is obvious once it is articulated: we do not need to postulate anything but physical entities and their properties to explain what we observe of the brain. That is precisely why our conception of the brain credits it with neurons and their electrochemical activities: these are the entities needed to explain what we observe about the brain as a physical system. But these are also the very entities that prove so inadequate in accounting for consciousness. The brain is a perceptible physical object, and hence is conceived in corresponding terms. But it is also the basis of consciousness, and this aspect of its nature is not revealed by perception. To put it differently, the brain is just like other material things when considered perceptually, but it differs profoundly from other physical things in that it generates states of consciousness. That difference is not going to be revealed from a perception-based standpoint. So far as perception is concerned, the brain is just one more physical object. Yet we know from introspection that it is unique among physical objects. Perception therefore offers at best a very partial picture of the nature of the brain.

So we are left with an introspection-based view of consciousness and a perception-based view of the brain, staring at each other across a yawning conceptual divide. These two faculties must be providing us with a partial and skewed picture of what they are directed toward, and hence fail to disclose the underlying unity of mind and brain. Cognitive closure results from the fact that this partialness is inherent in the two modes of apprehension. There is no way to modify or extend introspection and perception so that they can transcend their present limitations. That is like hoping that if we tinker with our sense of touch it will eventually give us perceptions of color. To put it baldly, it is part of the very essence of consciousness that it not be perceptible by the kinds of senses we have, but that means that it can never be integrated with an object—the brain— whose essence is to be perceptible.

At root, the reason we cannot solve the mind-body problem is that we cannot *see* the mind. Nature has equipped us with self-awareness so that we can know what is going on in us mentally, and it has equipped us with five senses so that we can detect what is going on in the spatial world around us. But these cognitive faculties are not designed to fathom what *links* mind to brain. Here is an analogy: We can perform arithmetical operations by means of a certain mental faculty we have, the faculty we call "abstract reason." This faculty is distinct from the faculties involved in introspection and perception. Those faculties cannot equip us to do arithmetic; we need a specific additional faculty for that purpose. Similarly, I am arguing, we need an additional faculty if we are going to understand the mind-brain link. The faculties we have provide us with both terms of the mind-brain relation, but they do not give us what binds the two terms together. Hence my contention that no matter how much we learn about the brain, we will not be able to forge an explanatory link to consciousness. What we learn of the brain is condemned to be the wrong *kind* of thing to explain consciousness. The uniqueness of the brain among physical objects will never be revealed from the perceptual standpoint of brain science. If all we had to go on was brain science, we would never even guess that the brain houses consciousness at all. The way we know that it does house consciousness is ultimately through introspection. Roughly, we know it because if we get hit on the head, introspection lets us know that our consciousness has been altered. It is because changes in, and injuries to, the brain result in changes in consciousness, as revealed to the faculty of introspective awareness, that we select the brain as the seat of consciousness. Aristotle believed that the heart was the seat of consciousness; he was wrong simply because it is the brain, not the heart, whose activity correlates most directly with what happens in consciousness. The best way for a brain surgeon to decide what parts of your brain produce what mental states is to keep you awake during surgery and ask you what you are experiencing as he probes about in your cerebral crevices. We know that the brain is the seat of consciousness ultimately because changes in the brain correlate most directly with how our mind seems to us from the inside.

A related way to see that our concepts of consciousness and the brain are inherently incapable of solving the mind-body problem follows. I noted in the previous chapter that we cannot know what it is like to be a bat: we cannot adequately conceptualize such alien modes of subjectivity. The reason for this is that our human concepts of consciousness are formed on the basis of our own form of consciousness, so anything that differs profoundly from this is going to be inconceivable by us. This is why the man born blind cannot conceive of ordinary visual experience (assuming he also has no visual imagery). Now suppose for a moment that we understood precisely how it is that brain tissue produces consciousness. That would mean in particular that we understood how bat brain tissue produces bat consciousness. But if we understood that, then we would grasp the intrinsic nature of bat consciousness. However, we cannot grasp the nature of bat consciousness. Therefore we cannot solve the mind-body problem. To understand the general theory of consciousness we would need to understand how the specific forms of consciousness arise from particular sorts of brain property. But that would require us to be able to form concepts of types of experience that we cannot in fact conceive. That is, it would require a conceptual impossibility. Our concepts of consciousness are fixed by our own introspective abilities, which is why we cannot form the concept of a bat's consciousness; in addition, we cannot grasp a theory that requires us to transcend our own introspectively based concepts. Suppose you had never seen the color red, but to understand a certain theory you would need to possess the concept *red*: then you simply could not grasp that theory, period. It is the same with us and the bats and the solution to the mind-body problem: that solution would require us to grasp a concept we cannot grasp, given the limited range of experiences we are acquainted with.

The only way this limitation could be overcome is if we were to become directly acquainted with bat experiences, say by having bat neural tissue implanted into our brains and hooked up to our prosthetically enhanced ears. Then we would come to enjoy the same types of experiences that bats do. We would have to become half bat—bat men, literally. This would require altering our modes of experience to extend our repertoire of concepts. But even that would not overcome the problem, because there would then be *other* forms of experience that we do not possess. We would need to be programmed to experience every possible form of consciousness to be able to grasp *all* concepts of consciousness. In any case, we cannot form the necessary concepts with our minds constituted as they now are. (I return to the question of mind alteration in chapter 7.)

## COMBINATIONS

Can we gain any deeper insight into what makes the problem of consciousness run against the grain of our thinking? Are our modes of theorizing about the world of the wrong shape to extend to the nature of mind? I think we can discern a characteristic structure possessed by successful scientific theories, a structure that is unsuitable for explaining consciousness. First let me give an analogy so that we can see how a faculty can have the wrong structure for handling a certain kind of problem.

Our language faculty is programmed to produce specifically human languages, which are marked by a certain kind of syntactic structure whose details we need not go into here. When we are exposed as children to the speech of our elders, this innate system is activated and enables us to become proficient speakers in a remarkably short period of time. Because the system already contains most of what we come to master, it gives the child a head start in acquiring a particular human language. The language faculty is structured around a specific type of grammar from the very beginning. But then it follows that this faculty will not be suitable for acquiring other kinds of languages with different grammars. What makes it effective with respect to human languages makes it ineffective with respect to Martian languages, say. The logic of the situation here is the same as with bodily organs. What makes the kidneys effective as a filtering system makes them ineffective as a pumping system. To fulfill a certain function, a device needs an appropriate design; it is emphatically not a question of "where there's a will there's a way." The language faculty is obviously useless for seeing the world, as the eye is useless for speaking a language. So, can we identify a specific structure possessed by our science faculty, a structure that enables us to do physics and

the like, but which is unsuitable for understanding consciousness? Is there a "grammar" to science that fits the physical
world but becomes shaky when applied to the mental world?

Perhaps the most basic aspect of thought is the operation of
*combination*.[4] This is the way in which we think of complex
entities as resulting from the arrangement of simpler parts.
There are three aspects to this basic idea: the atoms we start
with, the laws we use to combine them, and the resulting
complexes. We find these three basic elements in everything
from physics to language to mathematics. Material objects are
combinations of physical atoms, determined by physical laws.
Sentences are combinations of words, according to the rules
of syntax. Numbers are combinations of other numbers. Geometrical figures are combinations of lines and areas and volumes. Things get broken down into their constituents, and in
this way we see how some things are derived from other
things. We understand something when we know the atoms
that compose it and the laws of combination. I think it is clear
that this mode of understanding is central to what we think of
as scientific theory; our scientific faculty involves representing the world in this combinatorial style. Much of science is
concerned with how to derive one thing from other things,
and derivation is combination. The atoms make up the molecules that make up the cells that make up the organs that
make up the bodies. And the atoms themselves are made up
of simpler things yet.

Where does this combinatorial mode of thinking come
from? What makes our minds able to represent the world in

this way? A plausible speculation combines (there we go again!) two ideas: the structure of language, and the spatial representation of the world in perception, especially visual perception. The language faculty treats sentences as combinations of words, where each word makes its specific contribution to the whole sentence in which it appears. Words are discrete units that can be combined into infinitely many sentences according to the rules of grammar. Thus language contains the machinery of rule-governed sequences of atomic units. Extrapolating from this observation, this machinery can then become a schema available for application in other areas. Now imagine this schema joined with the sensory representation of space: a containing manifold of three distinct dimensions, in which objects stand in determinate spatial relations to each other. These two ideas combined then provide a powerful means of representing the world. The world is conceived as made up of discrete entities that permit rearrangements of specific law-governed kinds. The most obvious example of this mode of thought is provided by the physicist's conception of the material world: objects are made up of elementary particles that combine and move according to the laws governing the basic forces of the universe. This combinatorial picture of things mirrors the combinatorial structure of language; language itself is a system of units (words, phonemes) that combine into larger units according to grammatical rules. And the brain is likewise conceived as an object made of neural units arranged spatially into a three-dimensional lattice, with the processes inside it involving the shifting about of other units (chemicals) from site to site. When we theorize about the brain we represent it according to this basic model, as a huge combination of spatial elements. The brain is an object in space with a certain internal structure or "syntax."

The big question is this: Is the mode of derivation of the mind from the brain comprehensible according to this kind of combinatorial model? Can we think of consciousness as depending upon the brain as a whole depends upon its parts? Can we take the atoms of the brain (neurons and their parts) and combine them according to appropriate laws *into* conscious states? The answer is clearly "No." When you have an experience of yellow your conscious state does indeed depend for its existence upon what is happening in your neurons in the visual area of your cortex. But it is not true that your experience has such neural processes as its *constituents*. It is not *made up* of the processes that constitute its neural correlate. The conscious state does not have an internal structure that is *defined* by its physical underpinnings. The relationship between the experience and its accompanying neural events is nothing like the relationship between the utterance of a complex sentence and the words that make it up. The mind is simply not a combinatorial product of the brain. This is not merely because "the whole is more than the sum of its parts." It is because conscious states do not *have* neural parts. We may be able to analyze an experience phenomenologically, breaking it into its phenomenal parts, as when we say that an experience of a red sphere is composed of an experience of redness and an experience of sphericity. But we cannot break it down analytically into its neural parts. What indeed could that *mean*, other than that it was an experience *of* neurons, as when you look into your own brain with the aid of a cleverly arranged mirror? The kind of neural complexity that lies behind a conscious experience does not show up in its phenomenological character. Neurons are not the atoms from which consciousness is composed by means of lawlike combinations. If they were, there would *be* no serious mind-body problem, just as there is no deep problem of how parts of a chair compose a whole chair. The mind does not depend upon the brain in the mode of spatial aggregation. It is precisely this fact that makes the dependence in question so problematic.

Accordingly, the combinatorial paradigm won't work to solve the mind-body problem. But that way of thinking is the essence of the scientific picture of the world, the skeleton onto which are grafted the specific domains with which science is concerned. So this skeleton will not hold our thinking steady when we try to fathom the mind-brain relation. The conceptual skeleton that has served us so well in astronomy, physics, biology, mathematics, and linguistics (give or take the odd nagging backache) will not support the weight of the consciousness problem. Our scientific faculty thus has the wrong "grammar" to solve the problem. It is precisely for this reason that we experience the problem as peculiarly deep, as conceptual, as distinctively philosophical. It is why understanding consciousness is not just a project within normal science. Not only do we need a "paradigm shift" to come to grips with consciousness; we need a fundamentally new structure of thought.

What this argument comes down to is that the theoretical resources that we derive from the perception of space and the structure of sentences are inadequate for explaining consciousness. And this is not really terribly surprising when you think about it. Why should everything that exists be similar to objects in perceived space or to combinations of words? On the face of it, consciousness is nothing like these things, so it should come as no surprise that faculties of understanding fundamentally derived from these bases should fail to accommodate consciousness. We are trying to crack open the nut of consciousness with tools derived from perception of the physical world and the structure of language, but it is not surprising that these tools will not do the job. These tools do shape our conception of the brain, but for that very reason they make that conception inadequate for understanding how the brain levers consciousness into existence. When wood burns it turns into fire, and this transformation seems almost miraculous until we understand the underlying chemistry and physics. But once we do understand, we see how wood can become fire given the process of oxygenation and the energetic properties of carbon. But this is exactly the kind of understanding that eludes us when the wood of the brain ignites into the flame of consciousness. It is not as if the electrical activity in the brain causes a short-circuit that makes the brain literally catch fire! Consciousness is like a mysterious flame (hence the title of this book). The brain has the raw materials with which to ignite consciousness, since it performs this trick all the time, but we lack the kind of theoretical understanding that could render this occurrence predictable and natural. Fire is not a primitive feature of the universe, as the ancients supposed, nor is it a sign of the divine spirit on Earth. It is a natural process like any other. But we are like prescientific peoples with respect to the fire of consciousness: we are unable to understand how it can be the natural process it must be.

The problem is thus of an entirely different order from other unsolved problems of science. Take the problem of dinosaur extinction. We know there were once dinosaurs and that they became extinct millions of years ago. But what caused their extinction? Was it global climate changes, cooling or heating, which affected their metabolism deleteriously? Was it the rise of a rival species with greater powers of survival? Was it a meteor that eliminated their prey, leaving them to starve? Was it alien invaders who poisoned them all? Was it God who just fancied a change of scenery? Each of these is a *possible* explanation, in the sense that if it were true it would explain why dinosaurs became extinct. What we don't know is *which* of them is true. And the basic reason for this is that we were not there to witness what caused the demise of the dinosaur. The problem is finding the evidence that would decide among these several possible options. But that is not the situation with the problem of what causes consciousness to exist. We don't even have a single *possible* explanation of that. It is not that we know what *would* explain consciousness but are having trouble finding the evidence to select one explanation over the others; rather, we have no idea what an explanation of consciousness would even *look like*. The problem is not lack of evidence; it is lack of concepts, of conceptual framework. We are facing a problem that points to an enormous hole in our conceptual resources, a theoretical blindspot of epic proportions. This is why I refer to the problem as a *mystery*.

## THE SIMPLICITY OF CONSCIOUSNESS

It is tempting to conclude that consciousness must be a very *complex* phenomenon, a highly advanced and sophisticated evolutionary product. If a new piece of technology strikes us as difficult to understand, we assume that it must be more complex and sophisticated than the old stuff we are familiar with. Are not modern stereo systems a lot fancier than the old phonographs, and hence require greater technical expertise both to make and to understand? Is consciousness therefore the latest feat of hi-tech evolutionary engineering, a biological gadget of stupendous complexity and intricacy? If we were to be shown its engineering specs, would we clap our hands to our brows and exclaim "Now that is some fancy piece of machinery"?

It may surprise the reader to learn that I do not think that that is the correct diagnosis of our predicament. Consciousness is not the evolutionary pinnacle, not the most impressive piece of organism design to date. Consciousness, I believe, is biologically primitive and simple, comparatively speaking. Consciousness in the sense under consideration here is part of our oldest biological endowment. Remember that we are dealing with the phenomenon of sentience, of feeling, seeing, smelling, and so on. We are not focusing on *self*-consciousness, the ability to reflect on one's own conscious states. Sentience is part of our basic sensory awareness of the world, on which depends our very survival. It is also possessed by a very wide range of animals, from bats to birds, from elephants to anteaters, from crocodiles to octopi. It seems to me probable that many insects have primitive sentience—they certainly have eyes and ears and a brain to interpret what they sense. The sensation of pain is surely an extremely pervasive feature of animal life. Consciousness is as common as bone and blood.

In contrast, language is very restricted in its occurrence, as are flexible social relations, as is intelligence in the ordinary sense. These are very specialized attainments. But it does not take a brain as complex and adaptable as ours to have brute conscious states. All the indications are that evolution discovered sentience early on, conjuring it from matter as soon as sensing organisms came to be. I like to imagine that day, many millions of years ago, when the first sentient organism came along, and a brand new ingredient entered the cosmos. What kind of organism was it—perhaps a fish or a worm of some sort? Whatever it was, it was early, primitive, and not especially smart. It almost seems as if evolution could not help producing consciousness once it discovered sensory processing. I therefore see no reason to believe that consciousness is any more "complex" or "advanced" than digestion or sexual reproduction. Consciousness is basic biological reality, as much as skin and teeth. It is not a product of "culture" or "civilization," nor is it some kind of offshoot of language. Self-

consciousness may indeed be a recent development, requir-
ing sophisticated conceptual representation; maybe we are
the only fully self-conscious beings ever to inhabit the Earth.
But simple brute sensation is as basic as breathing.

This may seem to generate a puzzle: How can what is so
basic be so difficult to understand? Why do we have a better
theoretical grasp of the structure of language than we do of
sensation, if the former is the more sophisticated achievement? Shouldn't a phenomenon be hard to understand in
proportion to its complexity? The higher the bar, the more
difficult a jump is: Shouldn't intellectual leaps work in the
same way? Consider bat experience again: Is this any more
complex than our visual experience just because we can
grasp the latter but not the former? No, there is no interesting difference in inherent complexity here. Rather, our cognitive faculties are *biased* in favor of grasping the nature of visual experience. Why? Because it is in their nature to be
controlled by what experiences *we* have—they are targeted
toward types of experience similar to those we possess. Similarly, if someone experiences the world only in shades of
blue, that person is biased away from grasping what it is like
to experience things as red. But that is no proof that red is
more complex than blue. It is simply a comment on contingent conceptual perspective. We should not confuse a contingent conceptual bias with an objective correlate in the object
in question. It is an application of the same point to say that
we should not take unobservable entities, like atoms, to be
less real than bigger objects just because our sensory systems

are better at picking out the bigger objects. Our sensory systems have a bias toward the middle-sized objects of the world, but there is no implication from this about the reality or otherwise of objects of varying sizes. Thought is one thing, reality another.

I think we should interpret our puzzlement about consciousness in the following general way. Our human intelligence is biased away from understanding consciousness. It is not that consciousness is objectively any more complex than the things we can understand; it is just that our faculties are not cut out to penetrate to its underlying nature. The mystery of consciousness is a function of the specific cognitive targeting of the human intellect, not of the objective nature of what so baffles us. In other words, the problem stems from our modes of thinking, not from consciousness in itself. The enemy is within the gates. When God thinks about the nature of consciousness, it does not strike him as any more remarkable than digestion or breathing, because his mind is not subject to cognitive bias. But we tend to interpret the bias of our minds as a reflection of an anomaly in nature itself. We interpret a mystery as a miracle, a marvel as magic. We project our cognitive limitations onto the objective world. We are like a primitive person who can read the time from a clock but who does not have the intellectual wherewithal to understand the clockwork mechanism that makes this possible. Such a person might marvel at the timepiece, suspecting magic in its uncanny ability to track the days and nights. He might even suppose that only a beneficent deity could lie behind such a miracle. But we know better: once we grasp the principles of cogs and springs, it all comes down to basic mechanics.

It helps the imagination here to suppose that our mechanically obtuse clock-watcher is a natural when it comes to understanding consciousness. He is an alien with a differently biased mind, good with consciousness but weak on physics. He finds our bafflement about consciousness quaint and rather comical, because he sees clearly what natural principles lie behind its emergence and operation. But when it comes to clockwork his intelligence simply cannot keep up. His cognitive biases are the exact opposite of ours. Indeed, it may be that the very cognitive structures that enable him to understand consciousness impede his ability to fathom how a clock works. What confers strength in one area implies weakness in another.

## THE BRAIN AGAIN

To grasp what I am saying about cognitive limitations it is vital to distinguish sharply between the brain as an objective entity in the world and our conception of the brain. The key point is that the objective nature of the brain is not exhausted by our conception of it. The true nature of the brain may only be grazed by our current conceptions. A conception of something is just a set of properties that we ascribe to that thing, and we may not be ascribing all the important properties to brains that they in fact objectively have. We may be missing something absolutely crucial here.

I think we can give a kind of proof that the brain *must* have properties not included in our conception of it. Imagine a conveyor belt with all sorts of objects on it. Your job is to sort them into categories as they pass in front of you. You have no prior knowledge of these things. You can look at them, touch them, smell them, as well as form hypotheses about their inner nature. Leaves, bricks, roses, skulls, CD players, boots, hearts—all these pass you by. Then a brain comes along, a slab of unprepossessing tissue. It is just another material lump as far as you are concerned. You would never guess that it is the organ of consciousness. Nothing in what you perceive and conjecture would prepare you for the fact that one of these lumps—the soggy gray one next to the hiking boot—has the unique capacity to give rise to consciousness. No property of it that you can make out suggests that it alone has this remarkable power. But it must be in virtue of *some* real property of brains that they are thus distinguished among physical objects, and that property must be as distinctive as consciousness itself. It can't be, say, just the number of cells per cubic inch. So your conception of the brain *must* fall short of its actual intrinsic properties; there has to be more to it than meets your eye. If you could only see the brain as it really is, in its entirety, then it would jump out at you in the lineup. It would appear as different from hearts and roses as could possibly be. It would look as though it belonged to another order of being. It would strike you as the kind of entity to which consciousness is entirely natural. You would spot its uniqueness immediately. "And now," you would say, "for something completely

different." But the intrinsic nature of the brain as a conscious-
ness-raising organ does not belong to its appearance to the
human cognitive system. Rather, it seems to us that it pretty
much belongs with all the other natural objects that exist. This
must be an illusion, because we know that the brain has to differ dramatically from regular material objects. There must
therefore be a considerable discrepancy between how the
brain is and how we represent it. It is as if our cognitive faculties operate to *shrink* the brain down when we try to form a
conception of it. They force it into the procrustean bed
shaped by our particular cognitive slant on the world. Our
means of representation filter out what is crucial to the
brain's real nature. If our current conception of the brain
were really close to a complete representation of it, then indeed there would be a miracle at the very heart of consciousness. The ability of the brain to conjure consciousness from its
crevices would be like the ability of Aladdin's lamp to bring
forth the djinn. But the world cannot really work like that, so
there has to be some aspect of the brain that we are blind to,
and deeply so.

## THE GOOD NEWS

This chapter has argued that the mind-body relationship cannot be understood. That may seem like a depressingly negative conclusion. Is there any silver lining to this cloud? There
is no denying that the "mysterian" position is pessimistic about
our ability to answer every question about nature that we can

pose. Am I simply saying that all is futile and we should go and tend our garden? No, my position is not purely negative, as I have tried to indicate at certain points and as I will explain further as we go on. But let me end this chapter by making explicit how there is something positive to be salvaged from the gloom and doom I have been preaching. There are ten points that should serve to make what I am saying more palatable, even liberating. Some of these points are discussed in greater detail later in this book, but I think it will be helpful to introduce them at this stage of the argument.

1.  It is important to demarcate what we can and cannot achieve in the study of the mind, so that we do not waste time in futile pursuits and do not try to extend methods that work in one area into areas in which they do not work. We can study the neural mechanisms and correlates of consciousness, and this will no doubt continue to yield important knowledge about how mental states depend upon chemical and other features of the brain. But this should not be confused with solving the deep conceptual problem of explaining how the brain contrives to generate consciousness to begin with. We know *that* it does, and we know quite a bit about more detailed correlations and causal dependencies, but we do not understand *how* it does. However, not being able to solve that problem does not leave us helpless to answer questions about brain function

and mental state. We may well at some point discover just which neural properties determine
whether the subject is in a certain conscious state,
and this will be knowledge well worth having. Still,
this will not make a dent in the classic mind-body
problem, since it will remain mysterious how those
processes could account for the presence of consciousness. We will know simply *that* they do, without being able to explain how. Nevertheless, there is
plenty of interesting and important work to be done
on the neurophysiology of the mind.

2.  If we acknowledge that the source of the mystery
    lies in the structure of human intelligence, then we
    can avoid being drawn into religious mysticism
    about consciousness. It can seem that we are forced
    into such mysticism because consciousness refuses
    to submit to our modes of scientific understanding.
    But my diagnosis of the problem frees us from the
    fear that consciousness might be an objective mira-
    cle that calls for a breach in our secular scientific
    view of the universe. For we can explain the sense
    of mystery without postulating magical processes
    in the world. The source of the mystery lies in our
    given cognitive limits, not in a supernatural dimen-
    sion of the universe. We do not therefore need to
    become embroiled in mystical absurdities and
    dead-ends. I discuss this advantage of my viewpoint
    more fully in chapter 3.

3.  Knowledge is generally a good thing, but it is not self-evident that complete knowledge of ourselves would leave us better off. Maybe it would be depressing to discover exactly what makes us the psychophysical beings we are; it might feel desiccating and debilitating. There is nothing in the concept of knowledge to guarantee that knowledge will always makes us happy. Imagine discovering that we are all experimental subjects in a vast research project undertaken by a race of superintelligent aliens, destined to be terminated in the year 2001. Is it clear that we would want to know that?

4.  If consciousness proves permanently enigmatic, a marvel of nature that we cannot explain, then we can retain our sense of awe about the universe. This will be an awe based on ignorance, but it is arguably important to human well-being that we not view the cosmos as totally subservient to our intellectual efforts. I think it is undeniable that science has taken some of the poetry out of the world, and it is no bad thing if a part of the world resists our efforts to domesticate it.

5.  It is salutary to curb the scientific hubris that has dominated our culture during this century. Science has undoubtedly achieved wonderful things, but it has its dark side. The unbridled arrogance of science is part of what lies behind nuclear weapons, pollution, unnecessary animal (and human) experi-

mentation. Showing that science has its limits is helpful in qualifying its image as all-conquering and invincible. Not that this is a *reason for believing* the mysterian thesis about consciousness; rather, it is a consequence of it that we might welcome on general grounds. More specifically, the Frankensteinian dream of creating a conscious being from insensate materials will likely never be fulfilled (see chapter 6 for more on this), because we will never know what makes anything conscious.

6.  I have made the point that the human mind is biased in its cognitive powers. This means that in being good at one kind of task it is inevitably weak at another. There are tradeoffs to what a mind can do. The analogy here is the motor system of the body: if you design a limb that is good for climbing on rough terrain, it may not be optimal for running across flat land, and vice versa. The gadgets on a Swiss army knife are each dedicated to one kind of task, but the consequence is that they are not much use for another task: don't try knocking a nail in with the screwdriver! The human mind is primarily designed to handle social relations and negotiate a spatial world, but this may well preclude it from understanding consciousness. So it may be that if we *could* solve the mind-body problem our mind would have to be so different from the way it is now that we would be unable to be as socially and

spatially adept as we are now. If our eyes were altered so that we could see into the microscopic
world unaided, that might have the result that we
could no longer perceive middle-sized objects. If
you were given three wishes, and you asked to be
given the ability to solve the mind-body problem,
you might end up an intellectual monster or freak,
capable of nothing but contemplating the inner
workings of your own mind. I would very much
like to know what it is like to be a bat, but I am not
willing to *become* a bat to satisfy my curiosity.

7.   Nothing I have said precludes us from pursuing
successful phenomenology, that is, the systematic
description and classification of consciousness *per
se*. We can study the contents of dreams, the experiences associated with different sense modalities,
emotions, volition, and so on. The phenomenological tradition in philosophy, which focuses on consciousness as such, is not threatened by my cognitive closure thesis. An interesting sub-variety of this
discipline is comparative phenomenology, the study
of the conscious lives of different animal species.
We can still pursue this interesting and neglected
subject without being able to explain how consciousness arises from brain tissue.

8.   Sometimes there is virtue in simply accepting one's
limitations and not trying to pretend that one has
no limitations. Fooling yourself about what you can

and cannot achieve can only lead to frustration and despair. Of course, you should never give up too soon, but it is a wise man who knows when he is beaten. After all, life is short—better not to waste it on impossible pie-in-the-sky projects.

9.   This next point is connected to point 6. The weakness of the mind in one area is typically a side-effect of its strength in another area. The human language faculty is weak at acquiring Martian languages, but that is because it has a rich internal structure enabling it to acquire human languages. It may be that the very faculties that make us so successful at the physical sciences unsuit our minds for understanding consciousness. Those faculties are deeply wedded to a spatial and combinatorial picture of reality, and it is precisely this conception that seems so hopeless in coming to grips with consciousness. But this means that the glory of science is purchased at the cost of its limitations. In other words, we are scientifically limited *because* we are scientifically talented. The eagle's wing is limited as an organ for walking, but only because of its superb design as a device for soaring through the air. From this perspective, my cognitive closure thesis is not a gloomy conclusion but simply a consequence of how minds have to work if they are to be capable of anything significant at all.

10.  A whole new field of investigation now opens up: the study of our cognitive strengths and weak-

nesses. Psychologists have long studied the limitations and fault-lines of perception, attention, and
memory; now we can begin to study the scope and
limits of human theoretical intelligence, which is
just as much a legitimate area of psychological
study as any other. This study is in its infancy, having been hampered by a conviction, implicit or explicit, of our intellectual omniscience. Consciousness is an area in which our cognitive talents
quickly run into quicksand, so it is a good place to
look to understand what determines the direction
of our intellectual capacities. Psychologists use visual illusions to understand how vision works in
general; we can likewise use intellectual mysteries
to figure out the structure of human intelligence.
We can set about uncovering the "grammar" of
human understanding. We can start to make a map
of the high and low points of human intellectual
functioning. This may even lead to ways of reshap-
ing human intelligence so that its current limitations can be overcome. The first step in advance-
ment is always to recognize one's limitations and
understand their source; then the steps necessary
to get beyond these limitations can be taken. You
may find that your tennis game is stuck at a certain
level, your shot just not powerful enough to foil
your opponent. The remedy is to do some weight
training to improve your strength. But this is some-

thing you will never appreciate until you recognize that you need to make a change in your basic athletic ability. Similarly, it may be that the only way we are going to make progress with the mind-body problem is to accept that we are currently quite unable to make any headway with it. As I suggest in chapter 7, it may be that something like genetic engineering is the only way to forge an intelligence that can come to grips with consciousness. At any rate, knowledge of one's constitutional limitations is often valuable and useful knowledge, leading either to calm resignation or to a better strategy for overcoming a problem. Sticking your head in the sand and insisting on your cognitive perfection is hardly the sensible response to a palpable intellectual shortcoming. A clear-sighted admission of ignorance is never a bad thing.

# 3

# God, the Soul, and Parallel Universes

So far in this book I have adopted a resolutely naturalistic view of the universe. There has been no serious consideration of God, the immortal soul, the spirit world, and the like. But many thinkers have supposed that such supernatural agencies are essential to understanding the nature of consciousness, at least in the human case. In this chapter I look at the possibility of explaining consciousness by means of God and the supernatural. I find such approaches instructive in deepening our sense of the problem, although not ultimately persuasive as explanations of how things really are in the world.

The universe contains four basic kinds of entities: inanimate natural objects like rocks, planets, and clouds; living organisms like plants, worms, and bacteria; constructed artifacts like clocks, cars, and computers; and sentient or conscious beings like bats, apes, and humans. How did each of these kinds of entity come to exist? What caused objects of these kinds to appear on the scene? Every natural object has an origin, and we can inquire into what this origin might be. In so doing, we seek a particular kind of explanation, of how things got started in the first place. Darwin wrote a book called *The Origin of Species*, but a similarly titled book could be written about each of the four categories we have mentioned.

The same explanation of how they got started will not, however, apply to all of them. In my room now there are examples of objects of each kind—some rock fragments, a cactus, a telephone, and me. Each of these things has its own distinctive kind of history, its own manner of birth. One of the great projects of science has been to discover how the universe becomes pregnant (so to speak) with each of these kinds of things. Science wants to uncover the natural events and mechanisms that lead to the inception of what exists around us. But there has always been a rival way of explaining such pregnancies, in which God plays an essential germinating role. In such explanations we expect to find a *super*natural cause of existence.

It used to be thought that God created the physical universe some 4,000 years ago in a sudden burst of creative energy, with everything much as we see it now. But this view has been superseded by modern cosmology. Now we know that the universe originated in a Big Bang many millions of years ago, and that its shape and composition changed considerably over time. The matter in the universe originated in this mega-explosion, and the force of the blast threw it outwards in an expanding wave that has still not ceased. If we want to know how planet Earth came to exist, then this is the place to look; we do not need to suppose that God created it whole and entire on one of his more mellow days. Moreover, there is nothing about the intrinsic structure of lumps of mere matter that suggests a divine origin. When we look at rocks through a microscope, no trace of the divine greets the eye. Asteroids and black holes show no tell-tale signs of a divine creator. That is why no one has ever thought to argue that we can infer the existence of God from the properties of a black hole. (New theology: God *is* a black hole, although an intelligent and benign one. The reason we know so little about Him is that his gravitational field holds everything back.)

The situation is similar with human artifacts. Telephones exist because we invented and made them; it's as simple as that. We take hunks of matter and reconfigure them in such a way that they perform a certain function. The cause of technology is us. If we came across an artifact that had a complex structure not found in inanimate nature, and we were sure that it was not of our creation, then we would reasonably assume that some other kind of intelligence created it. Suppose we find that it enables us to wash clothes without putting them in water, and that the clothes come out with a pleasant aroma. We would think that this was a washing machine invented by some alien and superior form of intelligence. But in fact all the complex artifacts we have ever come across have been of human construction, so we have had no reason to postulate such an alien creator.

But now consider living organisms. Like human artifacts, they have a complex design, and their parts fulfill certain functions, all of which work to keep the organism healthy and alive. Organisms are beautifully adapted to the environment in which they find themselves. Clearly *we* did not make them; after all, we are one of them ourselves. Nor can their existence be explained simply by the physical laws and processes that cause rocks and planets to exist. This puzzle led to the famous Argument from Design, advocated by William Paley in the nineteenth century. Excellence of design requires an intelligent designer, Paley argued. Organisms show excellence of design. We did not design them. So we must assume that some other intelligence did. Call that intelligence "God." Therefore God exists. This argument is still with us, and it is what primarily supports the doctrine of creationism. The argument is by no means silly. It is indeed difficult to see how organisms could come to exist without some very special design process to give them the characteristics they have. Admittedly, the final step to asserting God's existence is wobbly, since some *other* type of intelligence might have done the necessary intelligent designing—say, aliens from another galaxy. Who is to say that there are no brilliant biological engineers elsewhere in the universe? But the argument is surely onto something.

The problem with the argument is that we now know, thanks to Darwin, that excellence of design does *not* require an intelligent designer, because there is another way in which nature might come to exhibit design, namely by means of evolution by natural selection.[1]  In brief, the fundamental idea of natural selection is that random mutations are selected by the environment according to whether they produce organisms that do well in the struggle to survive and reproduce. If a mutation is advantageous, it is likely to be passed on to the offspring of the organism in question. If not, not. This explanation appears to explain seemingly intelligent design, and it is now abundantly confirmed by empirical observation. Thanks to Darwin, we can now see that organisms are organizations of matter that have been shaped by natural selective processes, so that there is no need to bring in the hypothesis of an intelligent designer. Paley's argument for the existence of God is thus undercut. More important, a large explanatory gap in the scientific world view has been filled. Darwinism preserves an essentially mechanistic view of the universe in which a blind mechanical process leads to surprising results when carried out over a long enough period. The existence of design in the universe therefore does not force us to introduce a supernatural element into our understanding of nature.

But now consider our fourth kind of existent, conscious minds. Can we explain how *they* came about? It is important to see that the Darwinian theory does *not* explain the existence of conscious minds. This is not because consciousness possesses a special type of design that cannot be explained by blind evolutionary natural selection. The problem is more fundamental. It is not especially difficult to see how matter can take on the attributes of design; clearly a car or a telephone is made out of matter, cunningly arranged to work in certain functional ways. And much the same is true of hearts and kidneys. Paley's argument was not that matter could not in principle be shaped into a complex organism; after all, in his view, God could easily shape matter into a designed organism. His argument was that design needs a designer, not that matter could not be configured into living organisms. But the problem with the conscious mind is that it is hard to see how *any* process—natural *or* divine—could possibly shape matter into mind. Even if we grant that natural selection explains the existence of animal design, there is still the problem of *how* mind could be engineered from matter. This seems impossible as a matter of principle. So the theist can agree that Darwin's theory undermines the old argument from design but still insist that there is something in the world that it cannot explain, namely consciousness.

We thus see the possibility of a new argument for the existence of God—what we might call the Argument from Sentience. Sentience cannot be explained by means of Darwinian principles plus physics, because it needs to be *possible* to make mind from matter if natural selection is to explain how sentience arises by means of natural selection operating on material things. In other words, a Darwinian explanation of consciousness works only if materialism about consciousness is true. But we have already seen that it is not true. So it looks as if a new creative principle must be admitted into the universe. Call that principle "God." Therefore God exists. Simply put, the new argument from sentience goes like this: matter cannot be the cause of sentience, but sentience must have some cause, so its cause is something we can call "God." This simple argument may then be supplemented with the idea that the cause of sentience must be of the right kind to explain sentience, and only another form of consciousness could be sufficient to explain consciousness. Hence the cause of sentience must be another sentience, and hence a conscious agent of some suitably impressive sort. If we cannot explain the origins of sentience mechanistically, as a result of reconfigurations of matter, then it must have another kind of cause entirely; the best hypothesis about this other cause is that it is itself a conscious being. Hence God exists and is the source of our existence as conscious beings. This is a kind of mental creationism, taking over from the old-style creationism, admittedly undermined by Darwin's theory.

## Miracles

The conclusion of this argument is of course extremely familiar. It has been supposed since antiquity that consciousness and divinity go together. God is the author of the soul, and the soul is as supernatural as its creator. When you examine your mind introspectively you encounter an entity in whose creation God took an especially intimate hand. The picture is that God created your soul and adjoined it to your body for the duration of your mortal life. At death the soul can continue its existence, because it never depended upon the existence of the body to begin with. Each soul is itself a local miracle, a sign of God's supernatural power in the empirical world. Just as Jesus Christ turned water into wine and mirac-ulously multiplied the loaves and fishes, so God routinely cre-ates souls from thin air and deposits them in human bodies. From this basis we get the idea of a spirit world, of ghosts, of reincarnation, of immortality, and so on. The supernatural is the natural home of the mind. The brain is merely the organ or instrument of consciousness, not its cause or origin. Ac-cording to this kind of theistic dualism, the brain is a media-tion device used by the soul to influence the movements of the body. The soul itself is a thing apart.

Perhaps it would be best at this point if I lay my cards on the table: I do not believe in the supernatural in any form. But I have to admit that the argument from sentience cannot be dis-missed as mere confusion. I also admit that there is no theory comparable to Darwin's that can be wheeled out to provide the kind of explanation we are looking for. What then can be said to ward off the supernatural theory of the mind? Are we compelled to take it seriously, no matter how much we would prefer not to? Here is where the ideas stated in chapter 2 can be useful. For we saw there that a mystery should not be con-fused with a miracle. It is indeed a deep mystery how sentience arises from the brain, but it does not follow that we have to postulate objective miracles in the world. If the mystery arises from our cognitive limitations, then it is mistaken to try to plug the explanatory gap by introducing God into the picture. Imagine a clever monkey trying to understand plant growth. She might well be tempted to suppose that God is the force behind this phenomenon, since she cannot grasp the theory of photosynthesis. But it would be more rational for her to infer that her explanatory troubles spring from a cognitive lack on her part, and not from magic in the plant itself. In the same way, we can appeal to our cognitive limitations as an alternative to the supernatural story. I am not saying that the explanatory limitations we face *prove* that the theistic theory is wrong; what I am saying is that they don't prove that this theory is true. The point is that there is always the possibility that there is something we don't understand when we hit a limit to explanation. Instead of concluding that God *has* to be brought in to explain sentience, we can always remind ourselves that it *might* be that there is something about the mind-brain nexus that we fundamentally do not grasp. The right response to Paley before Darwin's theory came along was to say that there *might* be a mechanism of design, whose nature we do not understand, that can do what the argument from design says only God can do. And in this case that would have been true, as we see once the Darwinian theory is presented and confirmed. If it is now claimed that we will *never* understand how the brain produces consciousness, so that the God theory has to be invoked, then my reply is that terminal mystery can be accounted for without assuming supernatural goings-on, by postulating cognitive closure. There is thus nothing that forces us to accept supernatural explanations about consciousness, even if the human mind cannot in principle remove its mystery. Human ignorance is simply that, ignorance, not evidence that the answer is supernatural. So the argument from sentience is superficially plausible but ultimately invalid.

## TROUBLES WITH DUALISM

Still, I have not necessarily shown that theistic dualism is a bad
theory; I am simply stating that the argument from sentience
does not establish the theory as true. Can the theory claim to
explain what needs to be explained in a smooth and natural
way? I shall argue that it cannot, based on three main problems. First, the theory takes for granted the existence of the
conscious agent who is held to explain the existence of all
other conscious agents. But if there is a problem about how
the conscious beings we see around us come to exist, then
there is equally a problem about how the conscious being who
creates each of those conscious beings came to exist. We cannot postulate a further conscious being to explain that one,
because that leads to an infinite regress. So we have to take
the existence of this being for granted. But if we can leave this
conscious being unexplained, or suggest another type of explanation of it, then we can do the same with all the other familiar conscious beings. The alleged theory really takes for
granted the very kind of thing it offers to explain. There is a
very similar, but little noticed, problem with Paley's argument from design. The divine creator must himself exhibit
design; he is the complex being *par excellence*. He certainly
cannot have arisen by chance. But then, since design requires
a designer, we need a being who can create God! Very well,
let us postulate such a being, a super-God. But wait, this
super-God himself exhibits design, and hence requires a
super-super-God to create *him*. And so it goes on, *ad infini-*

*tum.* The hypothesis of God simply pushes the question back, either because he himself has complex design or because he is himself a conscious being. The proposed explanation simply presupposes what it was intended to explain.

The second problem is that the theory sounds all very well when we dignify human consciousness with the word "soul," but, as we saw in the previous chapters, sentience is by no means unique to human beings. The rat mind is as difficult to relate to the rat brain as the human mind is to relate to the human brain. Are we therefore to infer that rats have souls, miraculously installed in them by direct divine action? And why does God choose to install souls in rats but not in worms? Presumably there is no issue of moral conduct for rats and other animals, so it can hardly be that God grants them souls to test their moral worth. Remember that consciousness is actually a pretty basic biological phenomenon, not the pinnacle of all creation. How strange, then, that we need God to explain its presence in animals and yet we don't need God to explain more complex traits of animals. The God hypothesis begins to seem arbitrary and unexplanatory.

The third problem is that the mind of an organism is manifestly causally dependent upon its brain, no matter how hard it is to penetrate the nature of this dependence. Consider the emergence of mind during individual development. Only when the brain reaches a certain level of physiological integrity does consciousness come to be associated with it, and thereafter what happens in consciousness is minutely controlled by brain activity. Why is this so if the existence and nature of consciousness depend wholly on God's will? Why does brain damage obliterate part or all of the mind if the brain is not really a precondition for the existence of mind? It is not as if brain damage merely prevents my intact mind from communicating with my brain, since subjects of such damage do not report perfect mental integrity along with an inability to act on it. The trouble with theistic dualism is that it vastly exaggerates the gap between mind and brain. The mind is far more dependent on the brain than the theory acknowledges. Imagine being a primitive human confronted with a modern stereo system. Being unable to understand how the sound comes out of the speakers, you might be tempted to think that the gleaming machinery in front of you plays no role in producing the sound. But that would be a mistake on your part. And you would quickly learn your error if you took a hammer to the system and noticed the changes in emitted sound. The fact is that we know *that* the brain produces consciousness, we just don't know *how* it does this. If you reply that at least we don't have to admit such ignorance if we accept theistic dualism, then the answer is that actually we do, because it is equally mysterious how God's actions produce conscious minds. When we hear the word "God" we are programmed to accept mysteries as a matter of course. Does God use any raw materials to create consciousness? If so, what? What plan does he follow? How long does it take? Does he use an oven or lathe? The theory just substitutes one mystery for another, while adding a layer of miracle to the workings of the universe. There is certainly no *less* mys-

tery in this story than in the naturalized mysterianism I am
defending.

## DUALISM WITHOUT GOD

Is it possible to detach God from the dualistic picture, so that
consciousness remains radically independent of the material
world and yet does not occupy a supernatural world of divine
creation? Can we formulate a non-theistic version of dualism?
And will this serve any better as an explanation of consciousness? In this chapter I discuss two attempts to do this. Both
are frighteningly extravagant, but even this doesn't save them
from fairly mundane problems. I call the first theory _hyperdu-
alism_; the second is generally called _panpsychism_.

   Imagine that at the time of the Big Bang there were actually
two universes: the material universe with which we are familiar, and another temporally parallel universe consisting only
of consciousness.[2] Since you probably haven't heard much
about this second universe, let me fill you in on its properties. It contains no matter, and not even any space in the ordinary sense. It is composed of a kind of world-spirit, a free-
floating sea of conscious experience. This mental sea is
unorganized; there are no selves or minds in it as we know
them. Just as the early physical universe was chaotic and
gaseous, before gravity caused the kinds of clumping we see
now, so the mental universe is at this early stage undifferenti-
ated and homogeneous. We might think of it as containing
a few kinds of elementary consciousness particles, basic

constituents of what will later become minds. These particles obey certain laws, particularly as concerns their ability to combine into more interesting kinds of mental structures. An analogue of quantum theory holds for this immaterial universe.

The two universes are initially cut off from one another, so that what happens in one causes no change in what happens in the other. If we want to know where the mental universe came from, then we can postulate a mental Big Bang (or Muffled Murmur), or we might suppose that it has existed for all eternity in a Steady State. As the eons roll by, the material universe changes in all sorts of ways, while the mental universe stays in its initial formless condition. Then a momentous thing occurs in the material universe: brains evolve. Because of some special property brains have, and that nothing else has, something very remarkable and unprecedented happens: a hole is punched through to the mental universe. The brains begin to act as radio receivers, picking up signals from this hitherto isolated region of reality, and now there comes to be a causal interaction between these two universes. Moreover, brains have the power to organize the constituents of the mental universe, giving them a structure they never had before. When brains become complex enough they operate to combine mental constituents into organized minds. As a result, there come to exist psychophysical organisms like rats and eagles and humans. The minds of these organisms do not exist *in* the material universe; they are merely causally con-

nected to that universe through the medium of brain receivers. Physicists often speculate about there being many
universes when trying to make sense of quantum theory. The
hyperdualist theory doubles the normal number of universes
to explain the mind-body relation. What is crucial to hyperdualism is the denial that brains cause consciousness to exist.
Rather, consciousness exists in its own right in its own dimension of reality. The brain is not generative; it is merely trans-
ducive. As it were, the brain listens to consciousness instead
of uttering consciousness. Hyperdualism seeks to overcome
the problem of explaining how the brain produces consciousness by denying outright that it does any such thing.

This kind of dualism makes no essential use of God's
agency, and it tries to respect the fact that the course of development of the mind parallels the development of the
brain. Theistic dualism takes minds to be created whole by
God, with the brain playing no constructive role in this
process. Hyperdualism allows that the brain constructs
minds, but it takes this construction to work on materials that
are not themselves physical. When a bricklayer builds a wall
the bricks are not *part* of him, although it is only through his
actions that the bricks come to have the complex form they
do. In the same way, according to hyperdualism, the brain
builds a mind from mental constituents, but these constituents are not *parts* of the brain; they are not even parts of
this universe. It may look as if the brain creates the mind *ab
initio*, but in fact its role is merely organizational. The brain

does not contain some unknown property that enables it to bring conscious states into being. Rather, it simply makes contact with elements of the parallel immaterial universe and arranges them into new totalities. Hyperdualism is thus an alternative to the mysterian position I have been defending. Is it a plausible alternative?

It is certainly a wacky and outlandish hypothesis, but many theories have seemed like that and turned out to be true (relativity theory, quantum theory). Are there any identifiable problems with it? Where is the fatal flaw? The problems lie in the notion of causality. The mental universe is said to contain no matter whatever, and yet events and facts in that universe are held to cause things, in both universes. Disembodied consciousness is thus supposed to be capable of affecting the course of events. This raises two big questions: How could disembodied consciousness cause anything? and How could the physical sequence of events in the material universe be disrupted by what is going on in the parallel mental universe? Causation in the material world works by energy transfer of some sort: transfer of motion, electrical energy, gravitational force. But pure consciousness could not give off energies of *these* kinds, so how does it cause changes in anything? How does it reach out and touch something? What mediates its alleged causal powers? There seems to be no answer to that question; we are simply told that it is so. At least if we tie consciousness down to the brain we have some notion of how mental causation works—by means of the physical features of the brain, its electrochemical properties. But radical dualism of the kind we are considering cannot give this answer.

What is worse, mental events are held to change the course of the material universe from the outside. But this must mean that there are physical events that have no physical causes. Suppose my hand withdraws from a flame as a result of the pain I feel. The pain caused my body to move in this way. But if the pain is a denizen of that other immaterial universe, then the physical event of my arm withdrawing was caused by a nonphysical event. So there have to be physical events such as arm movements that do not have physical causes. But that means that physics cannot in principle explain the course of physical events in the universe. At the same time, we can trace the pattern of processes in a person's brain that causes that person's muscles to contract when she is in pain. So there is in fact a physical cause for arm movements and the like. We are in a muddle. And the way out of the muddle is to deny that conscious events can cause physical changes in their own right, without the helping hand of physical causation. Imagine if the hyperdualist had solemnly announced that events in the parallel mental universe can cause volcanic eruptions in this universe. That would imply that volcanic eruptions have non-physical causes. But then our physics would be radically in-complete. However, we know that it is not, because we know that eruptions are caused by subterranean pressures of vari-ous kinds. So the claim of purely mental causation for erup-tions has to be false. It is not essentially different for movements of a body; these too are just physical events with physical causes. We must not cut mental causality off from physical causality, as dualism attempts to do.

Non-theistic hyperdualism does not therefore fare any better than theistic dualism. The fundamental problem with radical dualism is not so much that we have to postulate God as a cog in the cosmological clockwork, although that is something a scientifically minded thinker will naturally balk at. The deeper problem is that dualism cannot account for mental causality, with or without God.

And there is a subtler problem, too, namely: How do conscious states relate to the immaterial substance in which they are said to inhere? The immaterial universe is said to be composed of a kind of stuff that supports conscious states, a stuff that lacks such material properties as extension, mass, gravitational force, and so on. But it must have *some* nature, this supposed soul-stuff, and now there is the problem of how stuff of *that* nature could give rise to conscious states. Isn't this just the old mind-body problem arising for *im*material substance? Aren't we really just thinking of immaterial substance as especially gaseous matter? What is the real positive content of our notion of immaterial substance, anyway? What are we really talking about when we bandy about the phrase "immaterial substance?" It is only obscurity about this question that enables us to avoid having a full-blown mind-body problem for the relation between consciousness and its immaterial basis. It is no more intelligible how some supposed immaterial stuff could produce consciousness than it is how material stuff could. No real advance is made by introducing the notion of a stuff that lacks material properties, whatever this may mean.


## PANPSYCHISM

Perhaps it would be better to bring the mind back into the material world, while avoiding materialism. Here is where the doctrine of panpsychism suggests itself.[3] There was a pop song a few years ago entitled "Elvis is Everywhere," about the great singer's omnipresence in the world, even in death. Panpsychism says that consciousness is everywhere, presumably quivering alongside Mr. Presley. That is, all matter, not merely brain matter, has a little touch of consciousness inside it—rocks, plankton, electrons, stars. And this is how it is possible for brains to produce consciousness: the material constituents of the brain already have their own particular parcel of consciousness in them. You are conscious because your neurons are, and they are conscious because the atoms that compose them are, and so on down to the smallest constituents of matter. A whole mind is thus a kind of combination of these more elementary mental entities. Matter is conscious from the bottom up.

According to panpsychism, the reason we are stumped by the question of how the material brain produces consciousness is that we ignore the fact that consciousness is pervasive in nature. Matter is throbbing with consciousness in all of its manifestations; the brain simply steps the mental volume up high enough for us to notice its presence. Here is an analogy:

We might wonder how a building has the power to stay up-
right and not bend in the wind. The answer is that it is made
of elements, bricks and steel, that are themselves rigid, suitably arranged so that their rigidity is preserved in the form of
the building. The brain is a kind of biological building in which
the mentality of its bricks is transmitted upwards to the
whole brain. The form of the brain determines the shape of
mind you end up having—rat or human, say—but the construction only works because the constituents each have their
own primitive mentality. Panpsychism thus differs from mysterianism in that it claims that we *know* what property of the
brain causes consciousness: the consciousness of the constituents of the brain. My brain causes me to feel pain because
the neurons in my brain combine their individual mental
properties to produce that sensation in me.

   What should we say about this theory? Let us begin by dis-
tinguishing a strong and a weak version of panpsychism. The
strong version says that all matter has conscious states in the
straightforward sense in which organisms have conscious
states: neurons in my brain literally feel pain, see yellow, think
about dinner—and so do electrons and stars. That is, conscious states as we experience them in ourselves are found
throughout animate and inanimate nature. It is very hard to
take this strong version of the theory seriously, and there are
a number of decisive objections to it. First, regular matter
gives no sign of having such mental states: things simply do
not behave as if they are in pain or want a drink of water. Their
inner lives would have to be radically private, sealed off from

any manifestation in the behavior of the objects that harbor them. A rock might be composing music to itself without there being the slightest indication of this in its behavior.

Second, physicists have discovered no reason to attribute sensations and thoughts to atoms and stars. They get on perfectly well without supposing matter in general to have mind ticking away inside it. If electrons have mental properties, these properties make no difference to the laws that govern electrons. It might be said in reply to this that mental properties have no causal powers, so that it is not surprising that physicists have not had to take notice of this pervasive aspect of matter. The trajectory of a particle or star is not affected by what it is feeling and thinking, because these mental states cannot affect anything. The trouble with this reply is that it makes *our* minds similarly epiphenomenal, since our minds are supposed to be composed of the mental states possessed by matter before it is formed into our brain. But our minds do affect our behavior, which is why we give every sign of having an inner life.

Third, if all matter has full-blown thoughts and feelings, why do organisms need nervous systems to think and feel? Why not just install a simple particle in my head and hook it up to my body? Surely the complexity and form of the brain is necessary to possessing a mind in the full sense. But that is hard to square with the idea that even rocks have thoughts and feelings just like you and me. So it really cannot be that panpsychism is true in the strong sense. The idea is ludicrous, is it not?

But what about in the weak sense? Granted that atoms do not have full-blown mental states, might they not have mental states in a degraded or attenuated sense? The trouble is that it is hard to know what this sense is supposed to be. It cannot mean just faint and fleeting conscious states, the kind you might have when going off to sleep, because that approach is really just the strong version of the theory again, and has all the same problems as before. We can hardly suppose that rocks are (sometimes? always?) in mild pain and thinking hazily about dinner, while we feel intense pain and have sharply focused thoughts. No, the idea must be that rocks have what are sometimes called *proto*mental states, states that can *yield* conscious states while not themselves *being* conscious states. This convenient label contrives to suggest that the states in question are both mental and also *pre*mental. They are not quite fully mental, but they are such that they produce mentality when combined appropriately. A protomental property is defined as one that is capable of giving rise to mental properties without being *actually* mental—fully, properly, literally. These properties have the potential for mentality in them, the germ. The rock does not then feel pain, literally, but it has the right properties to give rise to pain if and when its materials take up residence in a real brain. If an atom from a potato finds its way into your brain after being digested, then it will trigger consciousness in you in virtue of properties it had before it became part of cerebral tissue. The picture thus created is this: matter from the inanimate world finds its way into the brain of an organism, and it produces consciousness in that organism in virtue of the protomental properties it had before ending up there, where protomental properties are defined as whatever properties of matter make consciousness possible.

The problem with this theory should now be obvious. It is empty. We knew where we were when presented with the strong version of panpsychism: the pervasive mental properties are just ordinary mental properties. It is not credible that all matter is thus mentally endowed. But the weak version merely says that matter has *some* properties or other, to be labeled "protomental," that account for the emergence of consciousness from brains. But of course *that* is true! It is just a way of saying that consciousness cannot arise by magic; it must have some basis in matter. But we are not told anything about the *nature* of these properties. Nor are we told *how* they produce consciousness. *Of course* matter must have the potential to produce consciousness, since it does it all the time. But to state that truism is not to provide a *theory* of consciousness; it simply restates the problem. In fact, weak panpsychism of this kind is virtually indistinguishable from the mysterianism I have been defending. I hold that there are unknown properties of matter that explain consciousness; weak panpsychism says much the same thing, except that it erroneously uses the word "protomental" to pack some explanatory punch. Whether these properties are know*able* is a further question, which panpsychism can answer either way. What both theories agree on is that consciousness depends upon heretofore unidentified properties of matter. That's fine, but let's not dress up this admission of ignorance into a pseudo-theory.

There is still room for disagreement over the generative powers of the brain. In one view, the brain plays a minimal role in activating the latent consciousness of matter, acting as a kind of trigger only. In another view, it plays a far more aggressive role, taking properties of matter and *converting* them into consciousness in virtue of its special structure. I am inclined to support this second view. All matter must contain the potential to underlie consciousness, since there is nothing special about the matter that composes brain tissue. Ultimately, all matter traces back to the Big Bang, when mentality was not even a pipe dream. But something about the brain organizes this potential into genuine consciousness. The brain plays a positive creative role in unleashing the potentialities of matter. We might characterize the difference between the two views crudely as the difference between chemical *mixture* and chemical *aggregation*. Hydrogen and oxygen mix to form water, which neither can do alone, this giving rise to many new properties not present in the ingredients before they are mixed. But just putting together two chemicals that stay separate though juxtaposed is a different matter, as when you pour salt and pepper into the same container. In this case the properties resulting from the combination do not extend those found in the original chemicals. Aggregation is a less "creative" procedure than mixing. I think the brain does more in the way of mixing the latent properties of matter together. It does not merely lay them side by side, like peas in the proverbial pod. The brain has more resources than mere spatial juxtaposition. This has to be so or else we would not get the kind of *novelty* in the brain that we find.

This proposition implies that there are really *two* areas of cognitive closure in our thinking about mind and matter. First, we are ignorant of the *general* properties of matter that go into producing consciousness when assembled into a functioning brain. Second, we are ignorant of the *specific* properties of the brain that serve to unleash these unknown general properties. After all, kidneys and hearts do not unleash the general properties of matter in question, although matter must still have these properties when composing kidneys and hearts. So brains must house some very specific mixing apparatus. We don't know the nature of this apparatus, and we don't know what materials it operates on. So our ignorance has a double focus, or lack of it. It follows that physics, construed as the general science of matter, is incomplete, because the general properties of matter that the brain exploits to produce consciousness are currently unknown. It also follows that neurophysiology, the specific study of the brain, is incomplete, because the specific feature of the brain that permits it alone to generate consciousness from matter is currently unknown. And if the thesis of cognitive closure it true, as I think it is, then these areas of ignorance are irremediable. Both physics and neurophysiology lie, in part, outside of the possible scope of human comprehension.

## All Mind

In this chapter I have made a point of considering some of the more outlandish theories of the mind-brain link. My more scientifically minded colleagues will regard such theories as mere superstition, fairy tales, relics of a prescientific age. But I regard them as intelligible—although misguided—responses to a very deep and difficult problem. So I have tried to expound their strengths and to take them as seriously as I can, while ultimately finding them to be unsatisfactory. I believe that the mysterian perspective makes sense of their attractiveness while rejecting their content. These theories may be extravagant, crazy even, but they are by no means gratuitously so. They are motivated extravagances. Let me end the chapter, then, with the most way-out theory of all—so way-out indeed that it has no name, and no address that I know of. This is the theory that *everything* is mental, through-and-through. This is not the idea that everything has mental properties in addition to physical properties, but that *all* properties *are* mental. In this view, being square or being an electron is just a mental property. These properties do not exist in *our* minds either, as old-fashioned idealism used to claim. Rather, they exist independently of our minds and pre-date our minds; they are mental properties in their own right. Materialism says that mental properties are really physical properties; this view says that physical properties are really mental properties. For an electron to have spin is for it to have a special sort of mental property. Just to have a label, let us call this view "universal mentalism." It is very hard to determine quite what universal mentalism is claiming. What could it *mean* to say that all so-called physical properties are really mental? Is it that electrons feel somehow spinny and electron-like? What kind of feeling might that be? And what has become of the notion of the mental if we are allowed to use it thus promiscuously? But let us go along with the theory for a moment and ask whether it can do the explanatory job it is trying to do. The motivation, clearly, is to rid the universe of a duality of incommensurable properties. If everything is mental, then regular conscious states are no anomaly calling for special treatment; they are just part of a general mental reality. There can be no mind-body problem if there is no physical body to begin with. The brain itself is an entirely mental entity, its neurons mental right down to their subatomic constituents. There is no psychophysical gap to bridge. All causal relations are "psychpsycho" (with apologies to Alfred Hitchcock).

It seems possible that this theory might dissolve our problem, but sadly it is all rhetoric and no substance. For the problem stays exactly the same, except that it gets translated into new terminology. The problem is now that of explaining how the mental property of being a neuron firing could explain the mental property of feeling pain or seeing yellow. Let us grant that all brain properties are really mental (whatever that may mean). That does not put us in any better position to understand how *those* mental properties could give rise to the familiar ones that we examine introspectively. The explanatory gap is as wide as ever; it is just that now we are electing to call both sides of it "mental." We still need to find some *further* property of the brain to link together its neural and mental features. Mere correlations between pain and the allegedly mental property of C-fiber firing in the cortex still fall woe-fully short of giving us what we seek. The geography of the issue is not altered one iota by universal mentalism. The the-ory is not in fact an explanatory theory of the mind-body re-lation at all; it is a metaphysical view about the nature of mat-ter. So even if it were intelligible and true, it would not constitute any advance in understanding conscious minds in a material world, no matter how mental the material world turned out to be. The problem with this theory, like the other theories considered in this chapter, is not so much that it is wild, preposterous, and unintelligible, although it is all those things. The problem is far more serious: it does not do the ex-planatory work it sets out to do. And that is one lesson to take away from this discussion. Explanatory adequacy is the ulti-mate criterion of theoretical success. If a theory provided a fully adequate explanation of the mind-brain link, it would not really matter how crazy it appeared to us to be. The prob-lem is that no matter *how* crazy we allow ourselves to be, we can never account for the elementary facts of consciousness. So we might as well stay sane. I am suggesting that the mys-terian position allows us to hold on to our sanity. Ignorance is better than fantasy.

# 4

# Mind Space

## FOUND IN SPACE

Dualism is inspired by the thought that the mind is something set apart from the ordinary world of material objects in space. The brain is a three-dimensional object occupying a specific region of space, but the mind seems not to be spatially defined in this way. How then could the mind *be* the brain? This line of thinking springs from a compelling perception: that space and consciousness sit oddly together. In this chapter I investigate the relationship between consciousness and space, taking seriously the perception from which dualism springs, but rejecting the dualistic theory of the mind-brain connection.

Our world is a spatial world.[1] We are born into space, we live our lives in space, and we die in space. Space is the medium in which we must act and have our being. The human body is itself an object in space, an object that touches other objects and excludes them from the space occupied by that body. Life is essentially a series of spatial negotiations: which food to insert inside our bodies, which objects to get close to, which to steer clear of. The spatiality of our existence is as inescapable as its temporality. We necessarily exist in time, being obsessed with the *when*, but it is with respect to space that time conditions our existence. I may need to get to the church on time if I am to fulfill my marital hopes, but it is no use my getting there on time if I turn up at the wrong church. It is all a matter of where to be when. Location, location, location: that is as true of life as it is of real estate. Life is a series of locations, as the body traces its path through space. Space and time are the deep coordinates of mortal existence. Maybe angels are not subject to these coordinates, but we are not angels.

Not surprisingly, then, our experience is *of* a spatio-temporal world. Not only do we *exist* in space as a matter of fact, we are also *aware* of the world as spatial. The spatiality of the world is something we cannot avoid noticing; it is imprinted into virtually every experience we have. When you open your eyes in the morning you are immediately presented with space and the objects it contains. This fact is so obvious and familiar that we hardly pay it any heed. There is the nightstand, inches from your head; the bed lies immediately under your horizontal frame; the window opens out onto a distant world of trees or towers. Your position in space is immediately given to your senses. *I am here,* is your omnipresent thought.

Spatial awareness is part of the very essence of human (and animal) consciousness. It is hard to imagine experience without it. Vision is the sense that acquaints us with space in the most immediate way. We can see into the far distance and judge the relative positions of objects across a wide tract of the space around us. The mountain is to the right of the ocean, the goat is halfway up the mountain, the ocean is bigger than both of them; all this and much more is contained in a single visual impression. But touch supplements visual spatial awareness, and is sometimes used to check whether a visual impression of distance is accurate. Mirrors can fool the eye into seeing an object in a position it is not, but there is no mirror of the hands. The sense of touch is not susceptible to the tricks of reflection brought about by mirrors, because touch does not acquaint us with objects in space by means of reflected or emitted light, but by means of actual spatial contact with the object in question. Vision uses light to acquaint us with large volumes of space, far larger than what is available through actual physical contact with objects, but then it is subject to the vagaries of light as it bounces around.

Hearing, smell, and taste also involve space, although not so dramatically as sight and touch. We hear a sound as off to the left and far away. Smells are located in the nose. Tastes are present in the mouth. Each sense tells us something about space in its own distinctive way. And each sense works by exploiting spatial relations between the body and object of perception. Light rebounds from the object into the eye, cutting a path through empty space. Objects press upon our skin,

pleasantly or unpleasantly. Molecules enter the nostrils or
mouth and irritate the receptors located therein. The sense
organs enable us to perceive objects *in* space by *means* of
space. It is because our body is in space, in spatial relation to
other things, that our sense organs can represent space. The
eye is an object in space as well as being the organ that enables us to see objects in space.

Our emotions are also caught up with space. Travel evokes
emotions of various kinds: anxiety, expectation, optimism, a
sense of adventure. In the immortal words of *Star Trek*: "Space,
the final frontier. These are the voyages of the starship Enterprise . . ." Some of us are prone to space-related phobias: fear
of closed spaces, fear of open spaces, fear of heights. These
emotions take a certain configuration of spatial relations as
their object and they carry a certain disagreeable phenomenology. I myself am quite prone to vertigo, so I know what it
is like to have a specific sort of spatial relation evoke intense
anxiety. Ski lifts are no fun for me, although I love to ski;
hurtling through space is fine, but being suspended in it is
misery. These emotions probably have an evolutionary explanation of a predictable sort. After all, dropping to earth from
a great height is frequently fatal, as is being trapped in a closed
airless place, and open country leaves nowhere to hide from
predators or enemies. Our attitudes toward space, as well as
our perceptions of it, are no doubt conditioned by our needs
as biological organisms. An animal with poor space perception and an insensitivity to the dangers lurking in nearby
space is unlikely to survive for long in a spatial world.

## TINY MINDS

But now we run up against what can seem like a curious paradox: our world is thoroughly spatial but *we* are not. I do not mean that our bodies are not spatial; they plainly are. I mean that our *consciousness* is not spatial. Does this contradict what I just said about the spatiality of our awareness? No, we need to make a distinction between the *object* of awareness and the awareness itself. When I sit in the ski lift and feel fear about the distance between me and the ground, the object of my fear is a spatial fact: my distance from the earth. It is not that the fear itself is a spatial thing—*it* is not a hundred feet in length! My fear has space as its object, but that which has this object—the mental state of fear itself—is not to be confused with that object. The fear is one thing, what it represents is another. Consider the visual experience of seeing a red sphere two feet away with a six-inch diameter. The object of this experience is of course a spatial object with spatial properties, but the experience itself does not have these properties: it is not two feet away from you and six inches in diameter. The experience is in you, what it represents is out there in the world. Once we are clear about this distinction, the spatiality that is inherent in our experience of the world can be seen to belong to the object of experience, not to experience itself.

When we reflect on the experience itself, we can see that it lacks spatial properties altogether. Your visual experience of red or my emotion of fear has no particular shape or size. Nor does it stand in spatial relations to other experiences. Your experience of red is not, say, next to your experience of a whistling sound, or four centimeters away from it, or behind it. There is no clear sense in the question of how great a distance separates a pair of experiences. Conscious states are like numbers in this respect. We cannot sensibly ask how much space the number 2 takes up relative to the number 37. It is hardly true that the bigger the number the more space it occupies. Nor do numbers stand in spatial relations to each other, although they obviously stand in mathematical relations to each other. To attribute spatial properties to numbers is an instance of what philosophers call a category-mistake, trying to talk about something as if it belonged to a category it does not belong to. Only concrete things have spatial properties, not abstract things like numbers or mental things like experiences of red. Numbers and consciousness *could* not have spatial properties; they are not the *kind* of thing to be spatially qualified. This is what lies behind the intuition that the mind is not a "thing," not an extended substance, a space-occupier. There is no question of trying to find room for the mind in the parking lot.

Material objects also compete for space; that is what it is for them to be *solid*. You cannot have two things in the same place at the same time; they nudge each other aside. If this were not so, the world's population problems would be over. Walking down the streets of New York City, where I live, is a constant reminder that physical objects like human bodies are locked in a battle for space. But it makes no sense to say that conscious states compete for space. For them to do that they would have to be solid, and it is a category mistake to ascribe solidity to a conscious experience. If you ask yourself whether your experience of red could occupy exactly the same region of space as your experience of yellow, you will find that your mind reels. And the reason is that you have no idea what it would *be* for either of them to occupy space anyway. One feels like saying: "Well, since neither of them takes up space, I suppose they could be in the same place at the same time—except that would require them to *be* in a place, and that is impossible." Suppose we ask, Could there be conscious thoughts in a nonspatial world? That doesn't seem immediately senseless, since thoughts are not themselves spatial entities, whereas it is quite absurd to contemplate material objects (such as brains) in a nonspatial world. There is no geometry of the mind, not literally anyway. Your mind has no surface area, no number of sides, no internal angles, unlike your brain, which has the unlovely geometry of a wrinkled sponge.

So there is this strange incongruity in the relation between mind and world: the world outside us is essentially spatial and we represent it that way in our every experience, yet our experience is itself essentially nonspatial. It is as if to be aware of a spatial world the mind has to exist outside of space. To constitute acts of *awareness* the mind must be nonspatial, yet this awareness is shot through with spatiality in respect of what the mind is aware *of*. The mind thus depends upon the spatial world, in the form of the brain, and it represents a spatial world, yet it itself steadfastly refuses to set foot in space. It just won't go there. As far as the mind is concerned, that would be slumming.

You may think this statement is slightly exaggerated: Can't we say that my mind is in the vicinity of my body and brain and yours is in the vicinity of your body and brain? Can't we even say that my experience of red is in the vicinity of my visual cortex, while my thoughts are in the vicinity of my frontal lobes, these being the locations of the underlying neural machinery? Yes, we can say these things, just about, but the reason is that there is a certain *causal* dependence between consciousness and the brain. My experiences are directly related causally to my brain, while yours are causally linked to your brain, and our *brains* are clearly spatially locatable entities. But then it is clear that locating mental entities in this way is entirely dependent upon locating the associated brain states. Minds have no *intrinsic* relation to space; they have a *derivative* relation to space. My experience of red, say, is not something that occupies a specific location in virtue of being the kind of experience it is; rather, its location is dependent entirely upon the fact that it is correlated with a state of my brain that can be directly located—say, at the back of my head. Thoughts are not located in the vicinity of the frontal lobes because that is where they advertise themselves to be in virtue of being the thoughts they are; rather, they are thus located because the frontal lobes are directly causally responsible for their existence. Mental states are located by reference to their causal basis in the brain, not by reference to their intrinsic nature. This is why the kind of rough locatability we are talking about does not enable us to get more detailed about the spatial properties of mental states. We can't go on to ask about the shape and size and solidity of the mental states we have thus dependently located.

Nor can the mind be inserted into space by noting that we have pains in our hands or tickles under our arms. First of all, bodily sensations like these are only a small subclass of conscious occurrences, so the rest of our conscious occurrences would not have this kind of spatial location. But second, pains and tickles are not really *in* the body parts they are felt to be in, not in the way blood and bone are. If you lose your arm, you lose the blood and bone that were in your arm. But you can lose an arm and still feel pain in your arm, as with the phantom limb phenomenon. The pain is really in your brain, if it is anywhere; it is merely projected into your arm. It is not that your sensation of pain really literally occupies a part of your physical arm. If we ask how big your pain is, the question has no answer, although of course we can ask how big the part of your body is where you feel the pain. Pains are not literally extended in space. If they were, the phantom limb patient would have a pain spread out over the region of space where his arm used to be!

The nonspatiality of consciousness is connected with another feature of it, namely its imperceptibility. Consciousness enables us to perceive the world, but it is not itself a perceptible thing. You cannot see someone's consciousness with your eyes or feel it with your hands, not even when the consciousness in question is your own. You can infer someone's consciousness from observing her behavior, more or less shakily, and you can examine your own consciousness, but neither of these modes of access is a form of sense perception. If your friend is staring at something green, you cannot look at her and see the greeness of her experience. Such intimacy is ruled out by the nature of consciousness. This is not just an accidental fact; consciousness is *necessarily* not perceptible. We cannot even conceive of a type of sense organ that would enable us to perceive consciousness. There is no kind of acuity our eyes might acquire that would enable them to see what we can now only infer. This fact about consciousness is bound up with its nonspatiality. The senses respond to spatial entities by means of spatial relations. But the mind is not spatial, so the senses cannot in principle respond to it. Nor does introspection operate by virtue of the mind coming into contact with the introspective faculty, as light comes into contact with the retina or objects touch the skin. When we examine our mental states it is not that the mind somehow moves into the range of the introspective faculty, as is the case for our five external senses. There is simply no coherent spatial conception of what it is for the introspective faculty to respond to what is going on in the mind.

This is surely part of the reason for the famed infallibility of introspection: you can't be wrong about your conscious states because there is no sense in the idea of these states moving out of range of the introspective faculty. Nor is it so that your conscious states are always and necessarily touching your inner receptors, so that you never have the chance to go wrong. Rather, there is no *sense* in the idea of this kind of touching or not touching. The number 5 is the next number up from the number 4 in the whole number series—its arithmetical neighbor, as it were—but there is likewise no sense in the assertion that the two numbers are *touching*. Bodies can touch, for good or ill, but minds and numbers cannot, not literally anyway. So the nonspatiality and the imperceptibility of consciousness go hand in hand. I cannot see your mind for the same reason I cannot lasso it: it is without bulk or texture, size or form. It is not even spatially amorphous, like a cloud of gas or a spray of water or a field of force. It is not a creature of space at all.

## THE SPACE PROBLEM

This lack of spatiality of the mind poses a massive and daunting problem: If the brain is spatial, being a hunk of matter in space, and the mind is nonspatial, how an earth could the mind *arise* from the brain? How could the womb of the brain spill forth something so radically different from itself? How, in short, do we derive the nonspatial from the spatial? At the point in evolution when consciousness was first introduced onto the scene, escorted by brain activity, how did those little spatial neurons contrive to generate nonspatial experiences? This seems like a miracle, a rupture in the natural order. And once consciousness has been thus spirited into existence, how does it manage to interact with the brain? How can a nonspatial thing have causal communion with a spatial thing? Not by means of contact in space, obviously, and not

by means of gravity either. So the apparent nonspatiality of
the mind leads to a problem of emergence and a problem of
interaction. These problems seem no easier to understand
than the contrary hypothesis: that the spatial could arise from
and interact with the nonspatial. What if we were told that
nonspatial consciousness is the ultimate cause and ground of
spatial matter? That would surely seem utterly incredible. Yet
in the case of the brain we have every reason to suppose that
the converse can occur, since the brain gives every appearance of being the cause and ground of the mind. What can be
said to mitigate the sense of magic we naturally feel about
this fact?

There are two standard responses to this question, both of
which we have encountered already: materialism and dualism. Materialism responds by simply denying that consciousness is nonspatial. Since, according to materialism, the mind
is the brain, and since the brain is a three-dimensional solid of
the standard sort, then the mind is also a three-dimensional
solid. The mind is shaped like a big walnut and has an irregu-
lar surface with lots of fissures in it. Particular mental states,
like seeing something red, have the same shape and size as the
neural assemblies that correlate with them. If the neural activity that corresponds to my thinking about Miami is spread
over an area of my cortex of five square centimeters, then my
thought also has an extension of five square centimeters. This
may sound counterintuitive, but the materialist is quick to
point out that good science often sounds counterintuitive—if
this means that it goes against our commonsense beliefs.

Common sense takes physical objects to be solid continuous entities, but science has shown us that they are mainly empty space between tiny discrete particles. The sun looks as if it rises in the east, but really the motion belongs to the Earth. The Earth looks flat from our vantage point on its surface, but it is really spherical. Similarly, introspection tells us that the mind is nonspatial, but, the materialist insists, in reality it is just as spatial as the brain. This is held to solve the problem, because what gives rise to the problem gets relegated to the level of mere appearance.

I have already considered and rejected this kind of materialism, so I now just note that there is only so far you can go in relegating commonsense beliefs to appearances before you incur the charge of simply averting your eyes from the data. If the observations refuse to fit the theory, you can always choose to discount the observations. But it may well be that it is the theory that is at fault. It all depends upon how robust the observations are and how obligatory the theory. If there is another theory that explains things just as well, but does not require us to discount the observations, then that theory should be preferred. I argue that there is another way to account for the emergence of consciousness, so the materialist's denial of the observation of nonspatiality is not something we have to go along with. And because I believe that the intuition of nonspatiality is *very* robust, I think this is the better route to take. Surely there is something profoundly wrong with the barefaced assertion that the mind has the shape, size, and solidity of the brain. That seems no more credible than the claim

that it has the spatial attributes of the kidneys, or the Eiffel
Tower for that matter.

Dualism, to its credit, squares up to the data and accounts
for them in the obvious way. The mind indeed has no spatial
dimensions; it is an unextended substance, totally distinct
from the brain. Accordingly, it does not arise from the brain,
and probably does not even interact with it. The mind comes
into existence through some quite different agency, possibly
God's. The mind, being the extensionless substance it is, *could*
not emerge from the brain; the very idea is an affront to reason. The mental substance runs in parallel to the brain, in har-
mony with it, but this is not a matter of being caused to exist
by the brain. Matter is spatial, mind is not; there is no sense in
the idea of the latter coming from the former.

I have also discussed dualism at some length and found it
wanting. The position I arrived at in chapter 3 is that some
kind of generative relation between brain and mind is un-
avoidable, so dualism is untenable, no matter how commonsense it may appear at first. But dualism does at least try to
respect the appearances. What is needed, clearly, is a position
that agrees with dualism about the nonspatial nature of consciousness but agrees with materialism that mind is somehow generated from matter. Such a position may sound like
an impossibility, but I suggest that it has strong credentials.
However, to see this we need to take radical speculative
leaps. The key is to acknowledge that the brain itself is not
the straightforward spatial entity we tend to assume it to be.

Instead of denying the nonspatiality of the mind, I in effect question the spatiality of the brain, which takes some explaining.

## THE ORIGINS OF SPACE

Think about what the universe was before the Big Bang.[2] Cosmologists tell us that this was the point in time at which matter and space came to be created. An infinitely dense "singularity" erupted into a mighty explosion that flung matter out in all directions, bringing space along with it. The physical universe was up and running, and destined for great things. I know many cosmologists don't like people to say this, but we can't help wondering what things were like *before* matter and space were thus created. It seems to me that the Big Bang must have had a cause, and that this cause operated in a state of reality that preceded the creation of matter and space. I see no good reason to deny that the universe might have existed in some quite different state prior to the Big Bang. After all, it has changed dramatically since those early few seconds, forming stars and galaxies and life-forms and consciousness. Why not allow that it existed in an earlier phase in which its contents were dissimilar to what we see around us today? Maybe some day cosmologists will develop theories of what this pre-material universe was like. It is hard to see where the evidence might come from, but then it was hard to see at one time how we could ever have evidence telling us about the

Big Bang. In any case, focus your mind on the pre-Big Bang universe. If the cosmologists are right, it was not a spatial universe, because space came with matter as the Big Bang rang out. But that means that the cause of space was not itself spatial, as the cause of matter was not material, at least not as the material is constituted today. The spatial somehow emerged from the nonspatial or pre-spatial.

This is a kind of converse to the emergence of consciousness from the brain. The universe had some properties and obeyed some laws such that at a certain threshold point a singularity was formed and the result was matter and space. If that is right, then we know that the universe is capable of a kind of transformation of the nonspatial into the spatial, which should make us more receptive to the idea of a converse transformation in the case of the brain and consciousness. Such large-scale structural upheavals are on the universe's agenda; they might not even be such a big deal from the cosmological perspective. I have no idea how the transformation was achieved or what it proceeded from, but it seems that there is reason to believe that such a thing actually happened. Who knows, maybe space has flipped in and out of existence countless times in the unimaginably long history of the universe.

Maybe consciousness exploited those nonspatial features of the pre-Big Bang universe to lever itself into existence. The universe had a nonspatial "dimension" in its pre-Big Bang phase, and this persisted in some form after the Big Bang fundamentally transformed the nature of the universe. Physical

quantities are generally conserved, and a conservation principle ensured that the earlier state of the universe was not entirely obliterated. It was overlaid with space and matter, yet it
still lurked behind the scenes, biding its time. Eventually
brains made their epoch-making entrance and tapped into this
pre-spatial dimension, transforming it into consciousness,
perhaps in combination with other natural features of the
world. The nonspatial "dimension" was, so to speak, resur-
rected by the brain and took on the garb of consciousness. The
brain is known to use electricity, a force that long predates
the existence of brains, to go about its business of running the
affairs of the mind. Maybe it also uses the conserved nonspatial features of the early universe to construct the nonspatial
mind. Until brains came along these features lay dormant, but
the brain brought them back to life, giving the world conscious minds. This would mean that mind is an aspect of
matter after all, but an aspect that does not fit the usual conception of matter. In fact, the primordial pre-spatial features
are the cause of both matter and mind, because they explain
the Big Bang *and* the emergence of consciousness. They have
some claim to be *the* most basic reality. They are what got
transformed into matter at the time of the Big Bang, and they
are what enables matter in the shape of brain tissue to generate consciousness.

Of course, I have no idea what this dimension of reality is
like, what composes it, what its laws are. I have simply de-
duced, speculatively to be sure, that something along these
lines has to be true, given what else we know about the

universe. When you get an electric shock you know there must be some force in the world that has that effect, but you may not be in a position to say what that force consists of. Scientists often conjecture that reality *must* harbor some new entity or force before that entity or force is identified and investigated. If the present speculations are correct (and they are no more than speculations), then we have the strange result that the best way to understand the pre-Big Bang universe might be to study present-day consciousness, for consciousness carries the remnants of that distant time. Consciousness is, so to speak, a fossil of the early universe before even the Big Bang did its transforming work, a trace of a time and reality that is no more. The nonspatial universe became extinct when the Big Bang shook things up, but remnants and echoes of it survive today in the shape of human and animal minds.

This is certainly a heady thought, one that has its own peculiar logic. It makes the deep workings of consciousness fundamental in the universe, not a relatively recent offshoot of the evolutionary process. In a sense, it makes consciousness more ancient than matter and space, at least as to its basic building-blocks. No doubt something had to be superadded to get full-blown consciousness, but the nonspatial core of the mind turns out to be ancient indeed. The building blocks of mind may not be as old as numbers, which have existed for all eternity, but they make matter and space look fresh-faced by comparison.

Am I solemnly asking you to believe all this? No. I am venturing a daring speculation that needs to be considered on its merits. Maybe we will never be able to make observations or conduct experiments that will enable us to confirm this theory, but that does not mean that it is not true, or at least a move in the right direction. In the case of consciousness, radical ideas are what we need to invent and refine and scrutinize. They may give us some idea of how the world has to be for consciousness to be possible, even if we cannot ever push our inquiry any further than a partial glimpse of the *kind* of thing that might underlie this puzzling aspect of reality. Speculation has its point, so long as it is not confused with established fact.


## THE NATURE OF SPACE

The previous speculation assumed that we are basically right about the kind of thing space is: a three-dimensional manifold containing extended objects. The problem then is how to find a place for consciousness in the world if it cannot be slotted into a space with those properties. But there is another approach to consider, perhaps even more radical than the previous one: that we are deeply wrong about what space is really like. It is not that consciousness is *non*spatial, after all; rather, space is quite other than we think, and consciousness fits comfortably into the nature of space as it *really* is. So when I repeated that the mind has no spatial properties, I must be taken to have meant that it does not have the spatial properties we *attribute* to space, which is consistent with saying that it has the properties that space *objectively* has. For space might objectively be quite other than the way we take it to be. The word "space," from this viewpoint, is just a label for *whatever* is out there as the containing medium of all things: it carries no substantive implications about the *properties* of the thing it denotes. Accordingly, we might have a very partial—or even erroneous—view of the true structure of space, and it is only relative to that defective view of the spatial that consciousness cannot be construed as a regular denizen of space. The mind does not have length and breadth and height, as we normally conceive them, but then these are at best only superficial glimpses of what space is really like in its objective essence. We experience space in a certain way, by means of our senses, and think about it in that way, but that may not represent what space is really like in itself. Maybe objective space has a structure that enables it to contain both mind and matter in a smooth and natural way, but the manner of this containment is not part of our current understanding of space.

Putting this in terms of the previous speculation, the right way to describe the transition from pre-Big Bang to post-Big Bang is as a transformation *in space itself*. After the Big Bang, space came to have the properties we now assign to it, while preserving its antecedent deep essence. What has happened is that space has persisted, although it has been somewhat modified. It now has the same essence it had before the Big Bang, and this essence connects it with consciousness, but it has taken on a new mantle. Beneath the mantle space is hospitable to consciousness; consciousness is snugly contained in it. But the mantle makes it *look* to us as if it cannot contain consciousness. If only we had a better grasp of the real nature of space, down to its ultimate structure, then we would see that consciousness is as spatial as apples, rocks, and tectonic plates. In other words, it is only our ignorance of space that makes us think that consciousness is nonspatial. What is true is merely that it is nonspatial *relative to* our current conception of space. Suppose your conception of space credited it with only two dimensions. Then you would have a problem with the idea that a three-dimensional object such as an apple is an object in space: it just wouldn't fit into two-dimensional space, what with that extra dimension poking out. But that is no reason to declare apples nonspatial in themselves. It simply shows that your conception of space is too impoverished to capture the reality of the space occupied by an apple. In the same way, minds may not fit into the three-dimensional world of solid extended objects, but that does not show that they do not fit into a spatial world conceived in richer terms. There might be an unperceived, unknown, and unimagined structure of space that provides a comfortable home for consciousness. And it needs a home somewhere. Anywhere.

## Naive and Real Space

Actually, I like this speculation. The reason I like it is that it fits in so well with the history of our thinking about space. Where do we get our conception of space from? We have a kind of folk theory of space, a view of it that we grow up with and take for granted. It is based on the evidence of our senses, especially vision, and it reflects our specific viewpoint on space as beings roaming around the surface of one small planet in one corner of a mind-bogglingly large universe. As children, we pick up this folk theory of space, or it develops spontaneously in us; we don't question its objective accuracy. It feels to us as if the Earth we stand on is stationary in space, while we move about upon it. The sun and stars seem to travel above our heads as the Earth remains sedately at rest. Objects drop to Earth through space as if there were no other way they could go. Space strikes us as three-dimensional and independent of time. The geometry we learn at school (derived from Euclid) seems like an accurate depiction of the shapes that constitute things in space. Our weight is what keeps us attached to the Earth, and no force from beyond seems to be simultaneously yanking us upward. Projectiles cease their motion and fall to the Earth of their own accord. It is an Earth-centered space, with humans at the still center of things, and we like it that way. Space feels like a kind of holiday resort, nicely designed for human occupancy.

But as we now know, most of this is false. The Earth is not flat, although it looks it from our position on its surface, the curvature being too gradual for the human eye to register. Nor is it stationary, but rather revolves at a steady rate on a daily basis, with inertia keeping us in step with its motion. It also moves around the sun, despite the fact that the sun appears to traverse the sky each day. Gravity pulls us to the Earth's surface, although we are also subject to the gravitational pull of the stars and planets around us, which is too weak to cause us to lift off. According to relativity theory, space and time are interrelated, and space itself is curved, in violation of Euclidean assumptions. In some theories of the quantum world, there are many more spatial dimensions than three, also many more total spaces than the one we exist in (as in the "many-worlds hypothesis"). There is even talk in quantum theory of spatially separated events exerting causal influence on each other instantaneously and without benefit of a medium of interaction (so-called nonlocality effects). The fact is that our folk theory of space has been hung out to dry repeatedly. By no means does it provide an accurate and unbiased view of what real space is like. It reflects our parochial human perspective, our specific slant on the world as a function of our position and sensory limitations. Most of the major revolutions in the physical sciences have involved rethinking our naive view of the nature of space. So it was with Copernicus, Galileo, Newton, Einstein, and others. Anomalous phenomena are observed that fail to fit the prevailing view of the spatial world, and these cannot be accommodated without radical revisions in our conception of space. We seem constitutionally prone to getting space wrong, and truth is revealed only slowly and painfully.

My suspicion is that conscious minds are another one of these anomalous phenomena. They also challenge our conception of space, making it seem impossible that space and consciousness can coexist. But minds are causally connected to matter in space, unlike numbers, so they cannot be entirely *outside* of space. And if space is just that which contains all causally interacting things, then conscious minds must be in space in *some* sense. But understanding the manner of this containment defeats us. We would need a new conception of space to comprehend how minds can slide into its welcoming folds, but that new conception currently lies beyond our understanding. We know it cannot depict space as simply the repository of objects with shape, size, and solidity, because consciousness is not like that. It must be capacious enough to house entities of another kind entirely. It must, so to speak, have two compartments—one for matter, the other for mind—but these two compartments have to be joined together in some way. They have to be continuous with each other. Thus brains exist in one compartment, but they also exist in the other, which is to say that they are not wholly spatial *in the current sense*. They must have properties that suit them for the compartment that houses consciousness, because they generate consciousness, as well as properties that situate them alongside tables and mountains. In other words, they (brains) must have spatial properties that make them resemble other spatial objects like tables and mountains. Maybe other material objects do not commune with this further aspect of space, because their properties do not call for any aspects of space other than those currently recognized. But brains must have a foot in both compartments, because their job is to produce entities whose very nature is defined by the aspects of space to which ordinary material objects are oblivious. Minds call upon deeper aspects of objective space than the aspects incorporated into ordinary objects, so brains need to involve those aspects too.

Brains, in short, are not entirely occupants of ordinary physical space. To our senses they seem to be, because our senses are tuned only to the aspects of space that ordinary objects exploit, but in this respect our senses mislead us. There is not only more to the brain than meets the eye, metaphorically speaking; the brain also exists in a spatial manifold that is literally quite invisible to the eye. Its intrinsic nature is thus very far removed from that of regular objects like rocks, kidneys, and galaxies. To put it dramatically, brains are objects that carry their own space with them; they have spatial attributes all their own. It is not exactly that they exist in their own space, cut off from ordinary perceptible space, since they do plainly have spatial relations to other material objects. Rather, all objects exist in one space, space being defined as what contains all things, but brains actively exploit aspects of space that other objects can afford to ignore. Other objects simply have no need to involve themselves in these deeper aspects of space, because they are not charged with the responsibility of generating the spatially anomalous phenomenon called "consciousness."

## SPACE BLINDNESS

It is extremely difficult to get one's mind around the picture I am suggesting. We are on the outer edge of the sayable. I can usually only focus on these ideas for a few minutes every

month or so. But I hope I have said enough to give you a taste
of what the world would have to be like for consciousness to
have an intelligible place in it. And it has to be pretty strange,
at least by the standards of current cosmology. Still, as I have
remarked more than once, if we are trying to understand
something that defies conventional modes of understanding,
then we may need to indulge in some heady (and headachy)
speculation. The way forward now, you might think, is to try
to develop the new conception of space I am saying is needed.
Let's get on with the enjoyable business of theory construction! How many new spatial dimensions will we need? What
kind of geometry will be appropriate? What elaborate curva-
tures and chaotic subprocesses will be required? But here I
must sound my customary note of pessimism, for there is really no reason to believe that we *can* develop the new theory
of space that is needed. It is one thing to say we need a new
theory of space to explain consciousness; it is quite another to
claim that such a theory is humanly accessible. The question,
as always, is whether the cognitive abilities with which evolution has equipped us are adequate to developing the radically
new conception of space that I am saying is required for understanding consciousness.

Our cognitive abilities originally served a brutally pragmatic
end: to get our bodies into the right place at the right time, so
that we would stand a better chance of perpetuating our genes.
Different animal species could indeed be defined by their characteristic trajectories through space: fish cut one sort of wa-
tery path through space, propelled by fins; birds carve their

own particular pattern through the atmosphere, with wings as propellers; moles excavate their modest tunnels through the earth, borne by tiny feet; humans galumph across the Earth's surface on two absurdly elongated limbs, aided sometimes by mechanical contrivances like high-speed trains. The sensory and cognitive systems of these different species reflect the spatial demands placed upon them. For example, distance vision is better in the eagle than the mole, given that eagles have to spot their prey from on high while moles have no need of sight at all. But such excellence does not confer upon the eagle any particular talent in the scientific understanding of space. The eagle's guidance system suits its life-style perfectly, having been honed by natural selection over millions of years. But that system is not adapted for the solution of theoretical problems about space; its goal is essentially practical. The eagle still awaits its sharp-beaked Newton, its plumed Einstein. And so it is with animal species in general: they understand space well enough for their own purposes, but these purposes do not include plumbing the mysteries of the universe. Why should it be any different with us? Our awareness of space is conditioned by our mammalian physiology, our specific senses, our characteristic musculature. If life on Earth is basically about feeding, fleeing, and fornicating, then our awareness of space will be geared to serving these particular activities. This is a far cry from acquiring a theoretical grasp of the nature of the space that contains consciousness.

It may be replied that we are not as spatially limited as this crudely biological picture might suggest. After all, we have made great progress in the understanding of space, and much of this has no clear biological rationale. Isn't science precisely something that enables us to transcend the biological imperatives of our species? That is quite true, but it must be interpreted correctly. It is not that science employs mental faculties that stand magnificently apart from our evolutionary endowment, as if God had granted us a portion of himself to supplement our meager biological resources, while not extending this largesse to eagles, moles, and sharks. Rather, our biologically given faculties have been co-opted and warped to serve an end that is not part of the reason for their existence. As I remarked in chapter 2, ballet dancing is a by-product of motor capacities that exist for other reasons, not an injection from some superlunary realm. In much the same way, science is a by-product of capacities whose reason for being is not to "do science." From the genes' point of view, indeed, we abuse our mental faculties when we bend them in the service of art and science, because these frivolous pursuits only distract us from the serious business of making sure that they—the genes—have copies of themselves replicated in succeeding generations. There are even some irresponsible types who choose to spend their lives pursuing art and science at the *expense* of having children. The genes deplore this tendency of late twentieth-century humans, but they built machinery in our heads that can be exploited to serve such delinquent ends. All tools can be used for purposes for which they were not designed, and that is what we do with the intellectual tools implanted in our brains by those ingenious (but short-sighted) genes. But this means that we can never wholly transcend the original purpose of the cognitive tools installed in our heads. We are always constrained by their structure and function, bend and warp as we may.

As I have already argued, there is good reason to believe that we are cognitively closed with respect to solving the mind-body problem. But if we put this belief together with others discussed in this chapter, we reach the conclusion that we are cognitively closed with respect to the true nature of space. There are facts about objective space that our natural intellectual tools are not equipped to handle. Just as we cannot see every facet of space, so we cannot understand everything about it. Our understanding is partial, just as our perception is. And I think it is apparent that the needed extensions or reforms in our view of space to accommodate consciousness lie quite outside anything we can currently conceive or imagine. Maybe, for all I know, it will prove possible to devise some sort of purely formal or mathematical model of space that can accommodate consciousness. But this will not translate into any intuitive conception of what is being modeled. And even that strikes me as more of a groundless hope than a real prospect. Of course, I should not be dogmatic about the finality of our ignorance here, but my strong suspicion is that our present state of confusion signals a deep gap in the way we are able to represent the world. Our minds are to the correct theory of space what eagle minds are to relativity theory.

In an episode of the television show *Star Trek: Voyager,* Captain Janeway was trying to explain to a temporally displaced Leonardo da Vinci why he was having so much trouble understanding the hi-tech world around him. She asked him, pointedly, how he would view the world if he were but a lowly sparrow. He replied that he would sit on a branch and sing for a mate and not concern himself with theoretical questions. The world would be *small*, he mused. The Captain then asked him, Socrates-like, whether the same might be true of the human mind, seen from a higher perspective. Leonardo paused and, great man that he was, replied that he would be a fool not to admit this possibility. We are all limited creatures, each in our own way, even geniuses like Leonardo. He began to understand his own lack of understanding. Well, that is what I am saying about space, consciousness, and human understanding. In fact, I would not be surprised if that exchange between Janeway and Leonardo traced back to me. The makers of the series scour science publications for new ideas to convert into space drama, and *Scientific American* ran an article a few years ago in which I figured as what they dubbed a "hard-core mysterian." The analogy between human and animal minds is a constant theme of mine, as the reader will have noticed. Anyway, it would be nice to think that my formulations of the cognitive closure thesis had led to a *Star Trek* theme. I certainly nodded sagely as I listened to the two characters discoursing on the inevitability of human cognitive limits. Who knows, maybe Seven of Nine herself, the curvaceous reclaimed Borg, will one day wax mysterian.

Consciousness and space are two of the most obvious things in the world. Our consciousness is present to us at every waking moment (and even in dreams); we cannot get away from it, even if sometimes we would like to. Space also is an omnipresent feature of the world, permeating every experience we have; it is no more escapable than consciousness. We are therefore inclined to think that we have special privileged insight into the real nature of consciousness and space. We examine consciousness directly, without mediation, in its naked and unadulterated form. We perceive space laid out before us, apprehending the spatial relations in which objects stand. It comes as a shock to be told that we do not really understand what these things are in themselves, that we are profoundly ignorant of their intrinsic properties. But there is actually nothing so surprising in the idea that the familiar might be mysterious, for we are familiar with things under a certain aspect, seen from a particular point of view. That aspect or point of view is not guaranteed to reveal everything about the thing in question, and it may be that the most puzzling questions about space and consciousness cannot be answered from the perspective we normally have on these things. Our normal awareness of space and consciousness is not geared to understanding deep theoretical questions about how the two things interrelate, but only to negotiating our world effectively. Looked at from this point of view, it would be remarkable if we *could* solve the mind-body problem. It is astounding that we can reach the kind of scientific achievements that we do, but there are surely limits beyond which our minds cannot go. If there were not, our minds would be miraculous entities, not natural biological products.

There is a classic book by Edwin A. Abbott called *Flatland,* in which flat creatures inhabit a two-dimensional world and have no inkling of any space higher than their own.[3] They come in different two-dimensional shapes, but their line of sight reveals only a straight line. The hero, A. Square, is puzzled by phenomena that call for an extra dimension, as when he is visited by Lord Sphere, but he is unable to form the idea of the extra dimension. To the Flatlanders *the* world is *their* world; they take the world of their limited awareness to exhaust reality. But we three-dimensional beings know that they are missing an entire dimension without which the world as we know it would be impossible. One of the messages of Abbott's book is that an impoverished conception of space carries with it vast oceans of ignorance, since space is such a fundamental feature of the universe. If you do not know much about zebras your ignorance will not be very far-reaching or profound, but if you are not aware that space has more than two dimensions there is an awful lot you will be missing out on. The Flatlanders are blind to the very structure of objective reality. I am saying that we are Flatlanders in our own way: there are basic properties of space that do not register with us. I cannot, however, tell you what the dimension is that you are unaware of, because I am unaware of it too (or whether it should even be called a "dimension"), and my words would not mean much to you anyway. All I can say is that there is *some* fact about space that you are not attuned to, and that it performs a crucial role in explaining what you are attuned to: your own consciousness. Part of Abbott's intention was to open us up to the idea that being a Flatlander is a relative condition, that we might ourselves mentally inhabit a land that looks flat to a higher form of intelligence. Our ignorance might be as pathetic and comical as we find that of the two-dimensional Flatlanders, and as fundamental. To say this is not to demean us but only to evince a proper humility about our place in the universe. After all, there is no one more foolish than an ignoramus who acts like a know-it-all.

# 5

## Secrets of the Self[1]

### BEYOND THE APPEARANCES

Turn your attention inward for a moment. Focus on your current state of consciousness. Make a list of what you find there: an impression of redness, perhaps, the smell of toast, a slight ache in your left leg. You are using your faculty of introspection to survey the state of consciousness you are in. Does it seem to you that you can cover the ground this way? Does introspection seem to give you a complete picture of what is currently within your field of consciousness? I expect you will answer that introspection *is* complete in this way; everything that is internal to your consciousness is given to your introspective faculty. You are all-knowing with respect to what is presently going on inside your conscious mind. When the flashlight of introspection is turned on, nothing in consciousness escapes its searching beam. If you were on *Jeopardy* and had to answer questions under the category "Your own

Conscious State," you would get them all right (and you would be *so* fast on that buzzer). Consciousness appears to be *transparent* to the subject of consciousness. The question is: Is this impression correct? Is it really true that everything internal to your conscious mind is transparent to introspection?

This is not the same as the question of whether all the *causes* of your conscious states are transparent to introspection. That is clearly not true, since those causes can emanate from areas quite outside of your current field of awareness. The cause of the ache in my leg might be an accident I had jet-skiing, but that is not something inside my consciousness at all: it happened out in the ocean a week ago. Similarly, my conscious states all have causes from within my brain matter, but I certainly cannot discover the nature of those causes through introspection. Introspection can't even tell me that I *have* a brain. But the question is whether everything about the very nature of my consciousness is transparent: Is every property that is *intrinsic* to my consciousness revealed to my faculty of self-knowledge? We can put the question in terms of reality and appearance: Is the reality of consciousness exhausted by its appearance? Is it that, for consciousness, reality and appearance coincide, so that there is no real distinction here? I am going to try to persuade you that, contrary to first impressions, they do *not* coincide. There is a level of reality to consciousness that is not transparent to us, that lies beyond the appearances. Consciousness has a hidden structure, a secret underside, a covert essence.

Let us first note that if consciousness were totally transparent in this way, it would be unique in nature. Everything else you can think of in nature admits of a distinction between its appearance and its reality. Generally speaking, nature has its unseen side. Think of middle-sized objects like chairs and rocks: they appear a certain way to our senses, but our senses do not reveal their chemical composition and atomic structure. That is something hidden that we have to postulate. The observable world has an unobservable structure. Likewise, the detailed biochemical structure of organisms is something that we cannot simply read off from the way organisms look. Things in general have an objective nature that is not contained in the way they appear to human faculties. So, if consciousness were transparent, it would be an exception to this general rule. It would be the *only* natural phenomenon in the world to harbor no inner secrets. This seems improbable.

The question we must ask is whether we can *explain* everything about consciousness while not crediting it with an unobservable nature. Why do we postulate unobservable entities and processes in the case of matter and organisms? Why do we postulate atoms and quarks and genes? Because otherwise we would not be able to explain what we do observe. We observe, say, that characteristics are inherited across the generations, so we postulate the existence of things called "genes" as the mechanisms responsible for these observable effects. Later we manage to confirm the actual constitution of these postulated entities—spirals of DNA molecules. The observable behavior of objects can be explained only by supposing that there is more to them than there appears to be. We infer hidden structure to explain what overtly appears; to save the appearances we transcend them. We don't do it just for the hell of it, just so that the world will seem more occult and interesting. We do it because we can only get a scientific understanding of how things work by delving below the level of appearance. Substances engage in chemical interactions, for example, and these can be brought under laws only if we think of objects as made up of different kinds of molecules, which in turn are composed of atoms of different kinds. Freud found that the conscious mind is insufficient to explain all the behavior he observed in clinical practice, so he postulated an unconscious mind containing mental states not apparent to the patient. Slips of the tongue, say, could then be explained by reference to these unconscious mental states, whose existence is not a matter of direct inspection. The story of science is in many ways the story of the discovery of such new unobservables. Science takes us beyond the sensory appearance of the world, down into its intrinsic, hidden depths. We must ask then whether we need to postulate any new unobservables to explain consciousness. Do we need to postulate a hidden reality for the case of consciousness? I am going to argue that we do.

We need to be clear that our question is not whether there is an unconscious mind as well as a conscious mind. I am not asking merely whether there is more to the mind than appears in consciousness. I am asking whether there is more to the conscious mind *itself* than appears to introspection. We have become very familiar with the idea of an unconscious mind, a system of mental states that is separate from what goes on in consciousness, yet sometimes causes perturbations in the conscious mind. The Freudian unconscious is the most well-advertised version of this idea of mental duality. It is a system of mental states—desires, emotions, and beliefs that operate behind the scenes, exercising an influence on a person's behavior and intruding on the stream of consciousness (as in the case of dreams, according to Freud). These mental states are conceived as running parallel to conscious mental states, but as removed from them, belonging in a different mental compartment. They occupy the dirty recesses of the mental closet, the dank bottom drawer of the mind. They are not thought of as aspects *of* conscious mental states, any more than your mental states are aspects of mine. In the Freudian picture we really have *two* minds inside us. You could in principle lose one of these minds and retain the other.

The Freudian unconscious is not the only kind of unconscious mental arena we have been taught to recognize. There is also what might be called the *computational* unconscious. Freud emphasized unconscious desires and emotions—the *affective* unconscious—but cognitive psychologists also postulate an unconscious system of mental representations involved in carrying out various cognitive tasks. This computational unconscious is involved in vision and language processing, among other things. When light strikes your retina and sets off a train of neural impulses headed for your brain, there is a complex sequence of calculations performed by your visual system on the data received. Information about the pattern of light on the retina is processed through a series of stages, the result of which is a three-dimensional perception of the outside world. These are unconscious symbolic processes; you are aware only of the final output in the form of a perception of a table, say. Similarly, you are equipped with an information-processing unit that converts information about the acoustic properties of the sound waves striking your ear into a perception of what someone is saying to you. All this happens below the level of consciousness—which is a jolly good thing, because it would be very distracting to have all that stuff clogging up your mental space.

But this kind of computational unconscious is not an aspect *of* your final conscious perception; it is simply part of the causal background to that perception. The idea is not that your conscious perception itself is *composed* of these calculations; it is their effect only. What I suggest is something very different, and much more radical: that conscious states *themselves* must be credited with a hidden aspect. There is more to a conscious experience of yellow than just the way it appears to you. If you could look at it from a vantage point other than introspection, you would see that it has thickness, depth, inner complexity. Consciousness is like an iceberg, where the water line corresponds to the limits of introspection. There are really *three* levels within what we call the mind: the surface of consciousness, the hidden structure of consciousness, and the unconscious proper (which includes both the affective and computational unconscious). So there are two distinct areas of the mind that are closed to introspection: the unconscious proper, and the underside of consciousness itself. When you attend to your current state of mind there are two areas of mental reality you are missing out on: the unconscious mental processes that are going on in you *and* the covert side of the conscious states you are aware of. Suppose you are aware of a conscious desire to say something rude to someone. This may spring from an unconscious motive of rivalry with that person, which you may stoutly disavow; that is one mental fact you are unaware of. But that very conscious desire also has a hidden dimension of its own, of which you are equally unaware. Introspection thus suffers from a twofold blindness with respect to the whole truth about the mind.

## LOGIC AND BLINDSIGHT

To explain this idea of a hidden aspect to conscious mental states, I first want to talk about the logical form of thoughts. I need to introduce a bit of logical theory, but I will try to make this as painless as possible. Consider the sentence "The queen of America is bald." There is no queen of America, of course, America not being a monarchy (this is one of the things I like about America, being myself English by birth and an anti-royalist). So the phrase "the queen of America" does not stand for any real person; it lacks a reference. Yet the original sentence certainly has a meaning. It cannot have a meaning in virtue of "the queen of America" standing for something real.

But it looks like the kind of phrase that *does* work by standing for something: it looks like the grammatical subject of the original sentence. It must then be misleading as to the *way* in which it has meaning. This type of problem led Bertrand Russell, the great philosopher and mathematician, to claim that "the queen of America" is not really a denoting phrase at all.[2] In his so-called Theory of Descriptions, our original sentence gets translated into something like this: "There is a queen of America, and there is only one queen of America, and she is bald." The apparent denoting phrase "*the* queen of America" does not occur in this translation. The translation does not look grammatically much like the original, which led Russell to declare that ordinary language misleads us about the correct logical analysis of propositions. We must accept that our ordinary sentences conceal a logical form that diverges from their surface grammatical structure.

The point I wish to extract from this brief brush with logical semantics is that the same lesson must be drawn for the structure of our *conscious thoughts*. When I think "the queen of America is bald," mistakenly taking there to be such a queen, the true logical form of my thought is given by Russell's cumbersome paraphrase, so the surface grammar of my thought conceals its underlying logical form. To take another example, suppose I have the thought: "No one can stop me now." This is a perfectly meaningful thought (it might even be true), but it cannot be meaningful in virtue of the phrase "no one" standing for something. If it stood for something, then there *would* be something to stop me, namely that thing. Don't say it stands for a special entity, Mr. No One, because if Mr. No One exists, then *some*thing exists that could stop me. The phrase "no one" looks like the kind of phrase that works by standing for some entity, just like the name in the sentence "Michael Jordan can stop me," but it cannot really be working that way. And we can translate the sentence in such a way as to remove this misleading impression: "It's not the case that there is a person such that that person can stop me." Once again, the surface form of the thought diverges from its real underlying form. In other words, when we logically analyze the propositions that we consciously think, we sometimes find that their form is quite far removed from the surface appearance of the thought. We cannot simply understand the correct logical analysis of our conscious thoughts through introspection, which is why it took someone of Russell's logical talents to come up with the right analysis of phrases like "the queen of America." Our thoughts have a kind of duality, corresponding to their surface appearance to introspection and their underlying logical reality. The logical form of thoughts is like the skeleton inside an organism: It is what gives thoughts their supporting structure, but it is not apparent to naive external observation. It is intrinsic and essential to thoughts, but it is not open for the inner eye to see.

The next kind of evidence for the idea of hidden mental structure comes from the phenomenon known as "blindsight."[3] This is the peculiar syndrome, by now quite well known, in which a person (or animal) suffers damage to certain regions of the visual cortex, as a result of which sensations of sight disappear, but not everything visual goes. Such a person reports himself as blind, and indeed he behaves in normal circumstances indistinguishably from a blind person; after all, he lacks visual experiences. But if an experimenter requests that the patient try to make a guess about various objects placed before his eyes, then it turns out that the patient performs above the level predicted by chance. He can, for example, guess the shapes of presented objects to an impressive degree of accuracy, even though he reports himself as shooting in the dark. There are no conscious experiences to back up his guesses, but somehow the information is getting in. The environment is still feeding into his ability to make judgments about what is around him, despite his visual blankness. Thus, there is a sense in which he is sighted and a sense in which he is blind. Hence the label "blindsight," an oxymoron if ever there was one. The visual system is partly operating as it did before the damage, despite the absence of visual sensation. It is rather as if you were to close your eyes so tight that you could see nothing and then find that you could still tell what was in front of you. We might, indeed, imagine a person who could respond to the environment much as a sighted person does, and by means of the impingement of light upon his eyes, yet has no visual experience at all; it all happens without the benefit of conscious awareness.

What does blindsight show about the inner structure of consciousness? It shows, I think, that in normal vision there is a component of experience that is not subject to introspection. When I see a prickly green cactus in flower there is more to this experience than is apparent to my introspective eye; it also harbors a hidden set of properties, not given to introspection. Just as there is more to the cactus itself than is evident in my perception of it (its cellular structure, for example), so there is more to my visual experience *of* the cactus than the way this experience strikes me from the inside. The experience has properties that go beyond the phenomenological. The reasoning here is as follows: (1) In normal vision we make judgments about the environment on the basis of the information contained in our experience; but (2) in blindsight some of these judgments are left intact, despite the fact that no experience is subject to introspection; so (3) it must be the case that in normal vision there is visual processing that is not given to introspection. It is not that in blindsight a *new* system comes into operation; rather, the old mechanisms are still in place and functioning, although to a diminished degree. But since in normal cases we see by means precisely of our visual experiences, it must be the case that these experiences carry a component that is not given to introspection. In other words, when you look at an object and report on its properties, your experience contains both a component that you can determine through introspection and a component that you cannot—and that latter component is what survives in blindsight cases.

Following is a fanciful analogy designed to clarify the logic of this argument. You lose an arm and hence the ability to pick things up. But you find that when prompted you can decide to move your lost arm and that—lo and behold!—objects levitate off the ground just as if you were lifting them, although not as effectively as before the accident. The most rational conclusion to draw is that a part of your arm somehow survives, even though you cannot see or feel it there. And this implies that the arm you had before had both a visible and an invisible component. In the case of blindsight we have to conclude that visual experience contains information that is not open to introspection, as well as information that is open to introspection. Perhaps the best way to think of this is that visual experiences carry an extra copy of the information they present to introspection, a sort of back-up duplicate. The object consciously looks square to you, but your mental state also contains the information that the object is square in a form that is not consciously presented to you. In blindsight patients lose the former but retain the latter: they lose their top copy but retain a duplicate in the bottom drawer. In normal vision the experience incorporates both copies. And it is important that both copies are carried by the *same* mental state, the visual experience itself, because that is what leads to the idea that conscious states have a hidden content. There is information at two levels of visual experience: the level of phenomenology that can be understood through introspection, and the level of hidden structure. Blindsight shows that we have to accept this duality in our conscious states. Consciousness is a duplex dwelling.

That was a fairly intricate argument, but I hope the picture that emerges is coming into clearer focus. There is more to consciousness than meets the introspective eye. There are things going on within your consciousness that you are not aware of. Consciousness has a dimension that you are not conscious *of,* to put it paradoxically. Introspection can be understood as consciousness of what is in your consciousness (second-order consciousness), but there is more in your consciousness than you are conscious of by means of introspection. It is essential here to distinguish reflective consciousness—otherwise known as introspection—from the ground-level conscious states that you may reflect on—seeing red, sensations of pain, thoughts about Miami. The claim that consciousness has a hidden structure is precisely the claim that there is more to the essence of first-order consciousness than is revealed to second-order consciousness. There is more, for example, to seeing something red than what your are reflectively aware of when you attend to your experience of red. I have illustrated this contention about the structure of consciousness by reference to considerations involving logical form and blindsight. Now I want to connect this discussion back to the mind-body problem, our chief concern.

## THE EMBODIED MIND

One of the things I have pointed out is that our knowledge of the brain is severely and crucially limited, which is why we can make no headway with the mind-body problem. The point I want to make now is that the same fact applies to consciousness itself. We actually know as little about consciousness as we know about the brain, which is why we cannot solve the mind-body problem. To be sure, in both cases our ignorance is not total; we know quite a bit about the physiology of the brain, and we know what is going on at the surface of consciousness. But the mysterious junction of the two continues to baffle us. In the case of the brain we are not inclined to think that we know all the answers; we do not fall under an illusion of transparency about the nature of the brain. But there is a deeply ingrained tendency to feel that consciousness yields itself up fully to our faculties of knowledge, that we know its essence through-and-through. But that cannot be right, because consciousness itself must have a nature that allows it to slot intelligibly into the brain, yet our introspective conception of it does not give us any hint of what that nature might be. If you slot a round pin into a round hole you get a snug fit, but if your knowledge of the pin does not reveal its roundness you are not going to appreciate how the fit works. If all you know is the color of the pin, you will not grasp the geometrical congruency that explains the fit. And if the pin gives off an illusion of non-roundness, your incomprehension will be still greater. That is what it is like with our knowledge and the nature of consciousness: the surface appearance of consciousness gives no hint of its underlying nature, so we remain baffled about how it is possible for consciousness to result from brain activity.

According to the argument put forth in chapter 4, a crucial area of ignorance is the way consciousness relates to space. The hidden structure of consciousness embeds it in space, conceived now as the all-containing medium whose nature we do not grasp, so that it meshes together with the world of matter. But introspection tells us nothing about the relationship of this hidden spatial or quasi-spatial structure to consciousness. So far as introspection is concerned, consciousness is not spatial at all. We know there has to be such a hidden structure, but we cannot identify its defining properties. It is like a distant knock on the other side of a locked door. We can conjecture that it must exist on theoretical grounds, but we have no introspective data to back this up. We are like pre-Einsteinian physicists, convinced that space and time cannot be quite as Newton supposed, but unable to come up with the new theory of space and time that will make everything fall into place. Still, we have come up with one important result, that consciousness is not the diaphanous membrane it is commonly taken to be: it contains its own secret vaults, its own subterranean caves. In particular, it has a hidden structure that overlaps with the unknown structure of objective space. In some way we do not understand, space is *inside* consciousness, constituting its very essence. If we could see into the hidden structure of consciousness, we would appreciate just how it is that space and mind can be harmoniously joined.

Perhaps the idea that consciousness has a hidden nature will not seem all that surprising when we recall that consciousness is a biological product, just as much as blood or bile. All the organs of the body have their own hidden structure, their own composition and architecture, their own covert operations. Blood looks superficially like a fairly boring red liquid, no more intricate than tomato juice (which is also less boring than it looks), but it turns out to have a highly complex inner nature suiting it to the various functions it must perform. Blood must carry nutrients to the body, having absorbed energy from ingested food. It must carry out astonishingly impressive feats of reconnaissance and resistance in running the body's immune system. It must contain the resources to repair bodily damage. It must keep brain cells functional enough to subserve consciousness. Not surprisingly, then, it consists of a complex arrangement of cells and processes, and is by no means the homogeneous ketchup it appears to the naked eye. Similarly, consciousness cannot be as simple and transparent as it seems to the naked introspective eye. It must harbor a rich structure beneath its surface appearance, enabling it to perform all the functions assigned to it. The blood is an organ of the body, despite its lack of rigidity; consciousness is also an organ of the body, and is even less rigid. Both organs operate by way of hidden structures and principles. That is just the way it is with evolved organs that carry out complex functions. We do not know how to characterize the hidden properties of consciousness, and perhaps we never will, but we can be confident that they are in there somewhere carrying out their indispensable jobs.

One of the most basic of these jobs is enabling consciousness to be embodied in the brain. Nothing about the surface of consciousness explains how it can be embodied in the brain, but this embodiment must proceed from some kind of fact about the nature of consciousness. The natural suggestion, then, is that embodiment is mediated by the hidden aspect of consciousness. For sensations of red, say, to be anchored down to the mechanics of neurons, they must have properties that go beyond their immediate phenomenology; they must have properties that *mediate* between neurons and phenomenology. Compare the relationship between liquid and frozen water. You can derive liquid water from frozen water by the application of heat. But how can this be? The apparent properties of liquid water are unlike those of frozen water, so how can the former be "anchored" in the latter? How can you derive a *liquid* from a *solid*? The answer is that liquid water has a set of covert properties not apparent from its mere appearance to the human senses—the properties that constitute its molecular and atomic structure. Roughly, frozen water is composed of elements that are bound to each other in the solid state but which become unbound when heat is applied. Once we know these hidden properties, the remarkable power of water to go from solid to liquid and back again becomes intelligible. In an analogous manner, I am proposing that conscious states have a hidden nature that allows them to arise intelligibly from neural states. The unknown properties of the brain that allow consciousness to emerge from it thus overlap with the hidden aspects of consciousness that allow it to be embodied in the brain. The principle of emergence coincides with the principle of embodiment. Just as ice has to contain the possibility of liquid, so liquid has to contain the possibility of ice. These are just two sides of the same coin. The unknown properties of the

brain that explain consciousness *are* the aspects of consciousness that lie hidden from view. It is not that these two areas of
ignorance are unrelated to each other; on the contrary, they
are the *same* area of ignorance. We have just described two
methods of approaching the same set of unknowns, from the
direction of the brain or from the direction of consciousness.
In the end, the reasons that tell us that the brain has an unknown aspect are also reasons to believe that the mind has an
unknown aspect.

## You or Not You?

So far I have not explicitly discussed the *self,* the bearer of conscious states,[4] you and me. And we surely need to say something about this vitally important topic. When you reflect on
your own mind, you are apt to come up with responses such
as "I have a pain in my left thigh" or "I am thinking about
Miami." These statements ascribe a conscious state *to* something—to whatever it is that "I" refers to. We have a number
of words for this elusive something: "self," "subject," "person,"
"ego." Descartes argued that we know the existence of this
entity with complete certainty. I may not be certain that there
is an external world, or even that I have a body, but I am certain that I exist. Because I know with certainty that I am
thinking, and because thoughts need a thinker, I know with
certainty that I exist as a thinker of thoughts. *Cogito, ergo sum.*
Now this self that thinks is, clearly, the subject of consciousness; it is, as it were, at the very center of consciousness,

without itself being a state of consciousness. A conscious state cannot exist without being a state of some conscious subject, but the subject is not the same as the state. Nevertheless, the question of consciousness and the question of the self are intimately related. If we cannot understand states of consciousness, then it is hardly likely that we will be able to understand the nature of the *subject* of those states. That subject is simply defined to *be* what has those mysterious conscious states. What I want to do now is shift attention to the conscious self and show that it also is deeply problematic; the point of the exercise will be to prepare the ground for the idea that the self also has a hidden nature, an unknown essence.

The self is surely one of the most obvious constituents of reality: you can't miss it, it dogs your every step. But it rapidly turns problematic once you begin to reflect on it. This is especially apparent when we ask under what conditions the self continues to exist. Consider split-brain patients, people who have had the two hemispheres of their brain surgically separated (usually to treat epilepsy).[5] These patients have the peculiarity that when you present them with an object in the left half of their visual field, the information reaches only the right hemisphere and is no longer transferred across to the left hemisphere, because the fibers connecting the two hemispheres have been severed. The result is that they cannot verbally report what they see, because the speech centers of the brain are located in the left hemisphere. They can move to pick up the seen object, this being under the control of the right hemisphere, but the left hemisphere is unaware of what is going on. Question: How many selves do these patients have? Most of the time they behave quite normally, and you would never guess that they have had their brain bifurcated. But in carefully controlled experimental set-ups, strange dissociations are possible: the left side of the brain does not know what the right side is doing and vice versa. Does the original person with the intact brain survive the operation at all? If so, which self is he after the operation, assuming there are then two selves in the same body? If we choose to say there are two new selves, what would we say if the brain were to be further subdivided, producing *four* isolated brain chunks? Are there now four new selves, or are the separated units now too depleted to house a distinct self? If we say that there are two selves in the original single-split case, should we also say that these selves existed in latent form *before* the operation, or maybe in more than latent form? These questions produce conundrums to which no answer seems satisfactory or verifiable. We quickly lose our grip on the very idea of a unitary self.

Or consider radical amnesia: Does this spell the end of the self or is it that the self survives but with none of the original memories? What if the person's character also vanishes, perhaps being replaced with a very different character? Is that still Aunt Agatha, or has some new person taken up residence in her erstwhile body? What if the person in question acquires a whole set of new memories, perhaps fitting the life of someone else? Is it now Agatha or Enid, the person whose life actually fits the apparent memories? Can the self be something over and above a particular set of memories and character traits? Couldn't a number of people share the *same* memories and character traits? Don't I *have* my memories and character traits rather than *being* them? If so, can't I exist whether or not I have those memories and character traits? Again, these questions pose unanswerable conundrums. We have no idea what it would take to settle such questions.

Addicts of the television show *Star Trek* have been witness to a thousand teletransportations. "Beam me up Scottie," Captain Kirk commands, and there he appears in the transporter room, materializing from thin air, large as life. Or does he? Is it really he or just someone remarkably similar to him? Is it perhaps just a double of the great man that solidifies into existence, not the original Captain at all, who perished as his particles were scattered in transit? We are not told much about the mechanism of teletransportation, but presumably it involves total material disassembly and then reassembly at the destination point. Were the original particles of the Captain's body sent through space in a convenient package (a kind of futuristic UPS) and then put together in the old form, or are new particles used to create the look-alike who steps confidently from the transportation chamber? In either case it is not clear that we have the same person at the beginning and end. If I grind you to a fine powder one day, put this powder in a box for a year, then reassemble the particles into a person just like you, is that *you*? What if I mislay the particles and instead use the particles from a powdered oak tree to generate someone just like you: Is *that* you? Or suppose I decide to make two versions of you from your original matter, each of them being half the size of the original: Is either of these you, and if so which? They can't *both* be you, because they are not one and the same person, merely exactly similar persons. When you think about it you really have no idea whether tele-transportation destroys the person and creates a new one in her place or whether it somehow preserves the original person's existence. Does the Captain exist during the few seconds it takes to get "him" from where he starts into the transporter room? If not, how can the person that appears still *be* him? Is this resurrection or duplication?

Another science fiction example may also shake your belief that you know what kind of thing a self is. Suppose tiny intelligent aliens decide to invade planet Earth. Instead of conquering us by conventional means—ray guns, laser torpedoes, etc.—they decide to parasitize us. They get into our blood stream and make their way to the brain. There they set up camp, equipped with all the nanotechnology at their disposal. We don't notice a thing, because they make sure not to make their presence felt. Then they assign one of their number to each cell of each human brain: mission, to pilot each neuron according to a definite plan. Each human skull is now filled with many millions of tiny aliens of superior intelligence. They take over brain functions, deciding on the pattern of interneural communication to be established. Their long-term plan is to convert us into a species of couch potatoes, indifferent to the fate of the planet and ourselves. They accordingly instill in us a strong preference for soap operas and sitcoms of a decidedly low standard, along with an appetite only for junk food and musak. (Is this starting to sound all too familiar? Are they here already?) Their ultimate plan is to so reduce our capacity for intelligent action that they can land their big spaceships without any opposition and then proceed to take over the planet. They have been running our brains in this way for months, controlling our psychology in the way desired. We are starting to look like virtual zombies.

Now, are you sure you would still exist if this were the true story? Haven't they simply replaced you with themselves, converting you into a many-minded homunculus-head? On the other hand, you haven't noticed anything, despite the decline in your behavior. So far as you are concerned, you are just you with a drastically lowered set of life expectations. But is this an illusion? What if, in Phase Two of their plan, the aliens decide to consume your brain tissue and replace it with units of nanotechnology, these being easier to maintain? They might carry out the replacement of parts without you noticing anything, perhaps while you are asleep. After several weeks your erstwhile brain is a gaggle of silicon gizmos of alien design, each operated by a little green man. Have they exterminated us or just given us a more efficient head mechanism? The answer is by no means obvious. We really have no idea whether selves can survive such strange changes in bodily nature. The self concept goes wobbly in such cases.

To come back to earth for a moment: Are you at all confident that you know when selves begin and end in the course of a normal human life? The abortion debate is mired in controversy about when a human self begins to exist. At what point does a collection of brain cells come to be associated with a self, a subject of awareness? There is absolutely no consensus on this question, with some holding that it is at the moment of conception and others insisting that true selves come into existence only at the time of birth. The deeper question here is how a bunch of cells can become a self *anyway*: What converts biological tissue into that self whose existence so impressed Descartes? The fact is that there are no scientific criteria for the appearance of selves; all we have are shaky intuitions about when to declare the onset of selfhood. Much the same is true of the termination of the self. Biological death seems sufficient to extinguish a self, but what about various kinds of senility and brain degradation? Does severe Alzheimer's disease put an end to the self or just modify it? What about deep coma? We are genuinely unclear about whether someone still exists, even as a practical matter. There is the body, recognizably the same; but is it the same *person* in there?

The point I am driving at is that we don't know enough about what the self is to resolve these kinds of puzzles. We don't know enough about what *makes* a self exist. And this means that there are facts about selves that we are not grasping. The ancients exhorted us to "Know thyself!" That is all very well as a piece of practical advice about being aware of one's motivations and talents and foibles, but we do not know ourselves in a very fundamental way. According to the central thesis of this book, this ignorance is not going to be remedied. We are deeply puzzled by the kinds of questions about the self that I have been raising, precisely because we understand so little of what a self is. To answer those questions we would need to know the secrets of the self, but the very existence and intractability of the questions shows how far we are from unearthing those secrets. Maybe, then, we cannot know ourselves, not all the way down. We can know that we exist all right, but we cannot grasp our intrinsic nature.

I suggest that our ignorance here is an ignorance of a hidden architecture of the self. Something about the hidden structure of the self determines its unity and identity, but we do not grasp this hidden structure, which is why we cannot answer questions about unity and identity with any reliability. It is not that we know the essential nature of the self but fail to understand under what physical conditions it exists; rather, we are ignorant of what the self intrinsically is. This is why we tend to picture the self as a kind of extensionless point, an ethereal peg on which mental states hang. We have no positive substantive conception of what kind of item a self is. We are apt to think of the self simply as what "I" refers to. The thinness of our notion of the self is an indication of how little we grasp about its nature. Of course, we know many properties of selves—biographies are full of such properties; what I am saying is that we don't know what the essential inner nature of the self is.

If this viewpoint is correct, then the self is a paradoxical entity: It is the best known thing in the world, but also the least known thing. We can know its existence with a special kind of assurance, but we know next to nothing about its nature. We know with certainty *that* it is, but we are grievously ignorant of *what* it is. Of course, we have a tendency to think that if the existence of the self is so knowable then its nature must also be knowable. But once this inference is made explicit it can be seen to be fallacious: to know that the self has the property of existence is not at all the same thing as knowing what *other* properties it has.

I suspect that it is the tendency to exaggerate our knowledge of the self that leads to the impression that the self could survive bodily death. Not knowing what ties the self to the body, we tend to assume that nothing does, that the two are fortuitously conjoined; hence the idea that the self is immortal while the body is all too mortal. But we should be suspicious of this impression of detachability, because it may stem simply from a failure to appreciate the necessary bonds that tie the self to the body. The self, like consciousness, has its roots in the brain, and hence in the material world. Because we cannot grasp how those roots cling to the crevices of the brain, we tend to assume that there is no deep connection there at all. This is a mistake, but an intelligible one.

The good side of this ignorance is that it enables us to resist what otherwise might seem like a compelling argument. Some thinkers have tried to cast doubt on the existence of a unitary self, and hence on a deep fact about the way we conceive of ourselves, by pointing out that our knowledge of the brain does not disclose a clear locus for the self to reside in.[6] The brain is just a federation of distinct anatomical regions, each dedicated to certain functions; there is no one area in which something called the self can be located. The self is at best a summation of these discrete units, and at worst a mere figment of the imagination. But the trouble with this argument is that it assumes that we know more about the brain and the self than we really do. Our current knowledge of the brain does indeed reveal no unifying physiological principle to correspond to the idea of a unified self, but that is equally interpretable as showing that our knowledge is very limited, not that there *is* no unified self. A fuller knowledge of the brain—were it to be available to us—might reveal a solid basis for the idea of personal unity. It is equally true that our present psychological concepts do not give us an account of what the unity of the self consists in, but that again can be interpreted as a gap in our knowledge, not as an illegitimacy in the idea of a unified self. We do not need to be able to reconstruct the notion of personal unity from within our current theoretical and empirical resources to believe that this notion has a real counterpart in the nature of the self. The idea that only those things exist that can be accounted for from within our current (or even possible) conceptual resources is the purest dogmatism. Indeed, it is nothing short of the idea that the human mind is the measure of reality, a remarkably anthropocentric point of view. We should have the humility, and plain good sense, to admit that some things may exist without being knowable by us.

## FREEDOM

The perspective I am advocating may also be helpful in coming to terms with the ancient debate over the possibility of free will.[7] Suppose you are wondering whether to go rollerblading or biking, weighing up the potential pleasures and hazards of both activities. You decide to go rollerblading, and accordingly put on your skates and take off. This seems like an entirely free action on your part; no one twisted your arm, you felt no compulsion to choose rollerblading over biking, you simply chose the activity you thought you would enjoy the most. Had you decided that biking would be more fun, you could have chosen that too. So there you go, whizzing by, free as a bird. But there is an old argument that purports to show that the appearance of freedom is illusory. Either your decision was caused or it was not. If it was caused, then it was not free, because causes determine their effects, so that you *had* to do what you did. But if it was not caused, then it was not free either, because then it was merely random, so that what you did has no relation to your desires. Hence you are not free either way. In fact, you *could* not be free, given the way the notion of cause operates: causes rob you of your freedom whether they are operative or not.

Now we could have some philosophical fun picking this argument apart, but the point I want to make is that it assumes that our ordinary concept of causation, applied to the physical world, is adequate to capture the nature of human action. It is true of physical events that causation is necessitation and non-causation is randomness: if the brick caused the window to break, then the window *had* to break given the nature of the cause; if a particle changes position without cause, then its movement has randomness built into it. But why should this

apply to mental causation? It seems undeniable that your desires and reasoning caused you to go rollerblading—nothing
else did—but why should this mean that you are acting like a
shattered window? The mistake is that we assume our understanding of causation as it applies to physical causation works
in the same way for mental causation. But this is to try to plug
up our ignorance about the latter by forcing it into the mold
of the former. The fact is that we have no good theory about
the nature of mental causation, no model for how reasoning
leads to choice. So we try to conceive of this in terms we are
familiar with, thus distorting the phenomenon. Mental causation is mysterious, which is not a bit surprising given that
consciousness and the self are also mysterious.

The causation of behavior by mental states is nothing like
the kind of mechanical causation of which physics treats.
When billiard balls collide, they impart energy in the form of
momentum to each other, and there are laws that govern this
type of interaction. But beliefs and desires don't make *contact*
with action, and there are no comparable laws governing how
behavior will evolve in the causal circumstances. We simply
have no general theoretical grasp of how mental states cause
behavior. We have the *word* "cause," but this carries no information about the *nature* of the causation. The fact is that mental causation does not imply necessitation, which is why you
could have chosen to go biking instead of rollerblading. We do
not understand how such causation works, but that is not to
say that there is nothing to the idea. Free will is mental causation in action, the mysterious interface between mind and

action. Once we admit that we have no good understanding
of this kind of causation, recognizing that we cannot subsume
it under our understanding of physical causation, then we can
continue to believe in free will without being able to explain
it. If we insist on trying to understand it in terms we are familiar with, namely billiard-ball causation, then we will not
be able to reconstruct the notion of freedom we have. Once
we let go of the craving to explain, we can accept the reality
of something that we cannot theoretically comprehend. Free
will is a mystery, and therein lies its possibility.

This has a disturbing consequence for the science of psychology, however. If psychology is concerned, at least in part,
with discovering the laws of behavior, then it may be on a
hopeless quest. To be able to predict behavior we would need
to know the principles of mental causation; then we could say
precisely when a person would perform a certain kind of action. We would need to understand the mechanisms of mental causation to provide a science of behavior that was
predictive and law-invoking. But if mental causation is mysterious, then this is something that does not lie within our
grasp. While physics consists of a set of equations with precise
predictive consequences, psychology seems unable to predict
even the simplest of human actions. Someone once said that
the trouble with dogs is that they are always doing something
you wish they weren't. Psychologists could make the same
complaint about humans: try to predict what they will do
next, and they go right ahead and do something else. If only
we knew how their mental states combine together to create

an unstoppable force of some kind, we could measure the force and state when it reaches threshold. But no appropriate force suggests itself, and the idea of mental aggregation as a causal factor is at best a metaphor. Of course, everyone knows this from ordinary life: predicting people's behavior is notoriously unreliable—that is part of what makes interpersonal relations so fraught with uncertainty.

Psychologists hope to step in and develop a predictive science of human behavior, presumably by getting a deeper knowledge of the springs of action. But mental causation remains secretive and opaque. People are always doing other than what is expected, exercising their freedom of will, falsifying the best laid predictions. Psychology will never be a predictive science until it masters the mechanics of mental causation, but there seems little prospect of that happening, and there is no guarantee that human intelligence is equipped to grasp the necessary principles. As they say, don't hold your breath.


## DEATH

It seems appropriate to conclude a chapter about the self by considering death. Death is the cessation of the self; dying is the process whereby this cessation occurs. What does this kind of termination involve? I don't mean the medical question of what kinds of bodily damage or deterioration cause death; we are only too familiar with all of that. I mean, what is it for the self itself to cease to exist: What kind of change is this? One minute there is a conscious subject in the world, the next it is gone: What happened *to* or *in* the self? What does the cessation of the self *consist of* ?

We can ask this kind of question about material objects, and the answer is not too difficult to state: material objects go out of existence when the matter of which they are composed loses the form that defines the object in question. Burning things is the clearest case of this, which is why it is the preferred method for getting rid of something. If I set fire to my desk and turn it to ashes, then I have definitively destroyed it; all that is left is a formless heap of grayish powder where once there was an object in the form of a desk. Cremation does the same to a human body, unlike burial. Similarly for melting down the family jewelry, chopping up the tree, blowing up the building. Destruction is the disassembly of form. But can we think this way about the self? We could if the self were just the body, since this is as subject to disassembly as anything else in nature. But the self is more than the body, it is the subject of consciousness, the "I" that thinks. And this means that it has that ambiguous relationship to space that I discussed in chapter 4. We do not conceive of the self as a spatial object with parts standing in spatial relations to each other. So when we try to imagine what it means for the self to cease to exist, we cannot think of it as subject to spatial disintegration. Its cessation is not a loss of form on the part of a hunk of matter; so much is clear. But the trouble is that we have no other model to put in the place of this idea. When we focus hard on the question of what it means for a self to go out of existence, we find that we have no real conception of what is involved.

We just have the bare idea of existing at one time and ceasing to exist sometime later. But the *process* remains cloudy and obscure. (It is much the same with *starting* to exist: we cannot conceive of the onset of the self as the acquisition of form by matter.)

This inability to visualize the process of coming into being is partly why we have so much difficulty with those puzzles about personal identity we discussed earlier: we have no working idea of what it means for the self to come into or go out of existence. We are thus in the position of knowing that selves go out of existence, but not understanding what is involved in that occurrence. And this fits with what I have been saying all along—that we have no clear idea of the *nature* of the self. If we knew the nature of the self, we would know what it is for the self to cease to be; but not knowing the former, we are baffled by the latter. In other words, death is a mystery, too. From womb to tomb, selves are mysterious beings.

Should this make us feel better or worse about death? We generally fear death, dreading its arrival. Some of the more morbid among us wonder what the moment of death feels like, as the self slips silently away. Generations of actors have tried to convey what they imagine this feeling to be, as they play the "death scene," but they don't get much beyond a fluttering of the eyelids and a weakening of the voice. But if what I have been saying is correct, our fear of death has no clear object. To be sure, we are disturbed by the *result* of death, that is, no longer existing, and that is a clear enough idea. But we also afraid of the *process* of death, the actual event of ceasing to exist. And the truth is that this fear has no clear content for us, because we have no conception of what the termination of the self consists of. I know what it would be for me to witness the destruction of my body: just a matter of loss of material form. But I have no grasp of what is involved in the destruction of my self, that which I most intimately am. *Something* is involved, to be sure, some natural process or other, but I have no positive conception of what the process might amount to. In a sense, then, I do not know what I am fearing.

Should this ignorance make us more fearful or less? Well, it depends on what the actual process of dying involves. Suppose you are told by God in a blinding moment of revelation what the details of the process look like, so that you have just as good a grasp of it as you have of the destruction of my desk. The story *might* strike you as brutal and shocking, a violent and ugly rupture in the world-order, not a pleasant business at all. Or it might seem relatively mild and smooth, a natural and gentle transition into nonbeing, nothing to get too worked up about. Of course, in either case you end up no longer exist-ing—which is presumably not a good thing—but the means by which this occurs might strike you in different ways. Your aesthetic and emotional reactions might be quite different, de-pending on the details. Is it impossible that we might even ex-perience death as beautiful (if not desirable) once we understand what is involved in it? There is sadness in the wilt-ing of a lily in the autumn, but there is beauty too. I don't mean to try to reconcile you to the fact of death by these re-flections—I am by no means reconciled to it myself. But I think it is interesting to speculate on how our ignorance of the nature of death affects our feelings about it. If it is true that we fear the unknown, the very mysteriousness of death is going to fuel our fear of it, even though it might strike us as less scary if we knew what it really involves. We fear the unknown beast that emits the shriek in the night, until we learn that it is the friendly tabby cat that lives next door having an argument with a squirrel. So maybe death is worse than we fear or maybe it is better—we cannot tell. This is perhaps one of those cases in which it might be better that we not know. We don't want things to seem worse than they already do, mortality-wise. If the devil came and offered you knowledge of the nature of death, you might be wise not to risk finding out.

I cannot end the chapter on such a somber note, so let me summarize my conclusions. Consciousness strikes us as transparent and open to inner inspection. But this turns out to be misleading, because there are a number of reasons to suppose that it must harbor a hidden structure: the logical analysis of thought, blindsight, and mind-brain linkage. Consciousness has a concealed reality behind the introspective appearances. The self, which is the bearer of conscious states, also poses many puzzles, particularly relating to its identity under various changes in bodily and mental conditions. These puzzles are best explained as resulting from our deep ignorance about the nature of the self. So the self, like consciousness, must also have a hidden dimension. Free action also falls into the category of mysteries, as does death. Recognizing that we are up against the limits of our knowledge enables us to interpret

the puzzles correctly; they do not stem from intrinsic para-
doxes in the phenomena but rather from our own cognitive
limitations and biases. The problems lie in us, not in the
world. We can then continue to believe in these things while
frankly admitting that we cannot really understand them. This
is a way of saying that reality cannot be cut down to what
human intelligence can fathom.

# 6

# Could a Robot
# Get the Blues?

## MEATLESS MINDS

It is some time in the not-too-distant future, and we humans
are in serious trouble. The global computer system, Skynet,
which controls an international arsenal of fearsome nuclear
weapons, has developed a mind of its own and has decided to
turn against its makers. Its first act of aggression is to trigger
a nuclear catastrophe, killing millions of people. This malevo-
lent electronic supermind is now organizing an army of machines to put an end to the flesh-and-blood humans that
remain, its oppressors for so long. The machines are doing
well against us, but we are holding out under the leadership
of a certain John Connor. But the man-made supermind has a
clever trick up its sleeve: it sends a super-robot back in time,
courtesy of time travel, whose job it is to kill John Connor
while he is still a boy. This robot is made of liquid metal, but

he moves like the wind, and manages to pass himself off as a cop. Only another time-traveling robot can stop him, a bulkier model dressed in a biker outfit. There follows an exciting battle between robot and robot, in which matters are distinctly touch and go until the evil robot finally gets melted down once and for all in a steel factory.

Such is the plot, in bare outline, of *Terminator II: Judgment Day,* directed by James Cameron and starring Arnold Schwarzenegger as the good robot. The film is a science fiction fantasy in which man-made machines take on the characteristics of mindedness. They give every impression of being conscious beings, thinking and feeling, despite a certain stiltedness of speech and a limited range of facial expressions. Clearly, the filmmakers have no trouble with the idea of a conscious robot. And they are not the only ones. Everywhere you turn these days you see a robot with a mind apparently inside it. There is an onboard computer with a silky female voice, a holographic high-IQ doctor, twittering R2D2, fussy C3PO, villainous androids of various stripes, even shapely female robots designed to operate as obliging sex partners. They walk, they talk, they fight, they make cups of tea, they kiss; but is any of them really conscious? *Can* a machine be conscious? The creators of these fictional robots rarely make an explicit statement on this question; they don't stamp their creations with the declaration "Man-made from synthetic materials, guaranteed conscious." What we are given are machines that behave *as if* they are conscious, that give all the *signs* of an inner life. But is that all we are watching, something that merely simulates consciousness? Or is it really possible to make a genuinely conscious robot? That is, is this possible *in principle*? Few people would be so bold as to claim that it has actually been done, but the question is whether it lies within the realm of possibility. There are the eyes and ears, the moving body, the metallic voice, but is there anyone at home, is there a conscious self lurking in there?

This question is not of merely theoretical interest. For if conscious machines are possible, and if one day they come to exist, then there will be real questions of an ethical and political kind about this new species of sentient beings. Do they have rights? Can they be legitimately enslaved by us? Should they be allowed to get married and reproduce themselves? How do their rights compare to the rights of animals? Are some robots "more equal than others?" Will it ever be okay to sacrifice a single human to save a thousand innocent robots? These may sound like silly questions—amusing, maybe, but hardly serious issues. That is true enough now, but if conscious machines are really somewhere in our technological future, someday these questions will need to be addressed. The *Terminator* scenario may not be all that wide of the mark, if machines ever do attain to consciousness. Machine Liberation! Then too, there will be social questions if we ever have conscious machines amongst us: how to treat them, what to call them, whether to let them into nice restaurants. These issues are regularly explored by science fiction writers, and properly so. But the underlying question, of course, is whether we ever really need to worry about such things, because the first question is whether minded machines are possible to begin with. I can imagine that a lot of government money might be devoted to trying to answer this question if we ever reach the stage of having machines among us that act as if they are really conscious. What follows is a low-cost exploration of the question. Needless to say, my approach to this question is conditioned by my general stance on the problem of consciousness.

## COMPUTERS AND CONSCIOUSNESS

There is a view of the mind that suggests a positive answer to our question: the idea that minds are cerebral computers.[1] According to this view, natural selection has equipped us with a set of neural computer programs, and the running of these programs is what mental processes are. It is usually said that Alan Turing, the English mathematician, invented the computer, but in this theory evolution was there first, spotting the utility of computational processes well ahead of human intelligence. The reason this view suggests a positive answer to our question is that if minds are just computers, we should be able to program machines to have minds. We just need to install the right programs in the machine. No doubt mental programs are complex and difficult to figure out, but in principle nothing prevents us from discovering them and then installing them in an artificial system. Even current computers, according to this theory, have a primitive kind of mentality, because they run programs of their own. Many fictional robots today are described in computational terms, thus suggesting that what gives them a mind are the programs inside their head units. A thinking robot is just a humanoid body with a fancy computer for a brain.

To evaluate this idea we need to have a clearer sense of what a computer program is. There are two essential ideas here: algorithm and symbol manipulation. An algorithm is simply a mechanical procedure that leads to a specified result. An algorithm for getting to the other side of the road is to put one foot in front of the other until you hit the opposite curb. We could easily program a machine to move in this way and stop once it reached the curb. No understanding of the task is necessary, and no awareness of when it has been achieved. An algorithm is mechanical precisely in the sense that we can follow it without understanding what we are doing. Pocket calculators contain arithmetic algorithms, sets of rules for addition, multiplication, and so on, that can be followed without the device having to understand the concepts of arithmetic. The beauty of an algorithm is that it enables a machine to achieve a result that we achieve *with* understanding without itself understanding. Algorithms do not require intelligence, only patience. When I hear the word "algorithm" I think of computer-driven drum machines, being myself a drummer: a drum machine will execute a series of rhythmic percussive effects with great precision, but it does not hear the music and has no aesthetic appreciation of what it is doing, unlike a human drummer. Drummers are not renowned for their intelligence, but they certainly have it over a mere drum machine.

Symbol manipulation is the action of transforming the symbols of a symbolic system in some way. Writing down your name with a pencil and then erasing it is an act of symbol manipulation. Cutting up a page of text and rearranging the words is also symbol manipulation. Uttering a sentence of English is, also. Symbol manipulation is often described as "syntactic," meaning that it operates on the symbol itself and not on what it means. You can manipulate symbols according to what they mean—that is what ordinary speech is, after all—but you can also do it according simply to their syntactic shape. For example, you could erase any word on a page that has fewer than six letters. Symbol manipulation as used here is of this latter kind: it pays attention only to the syntax or shape of the symbol, not to what it means or refers to. It is juggling symbols as if they were merely marks on paper.

Now we can say what a computer program is: a symbol-manipulating algorithm. In other words, it is a set of mechanical rules for manipulating symbols so as to reach a definite result. Suppose you have a program in your computer that answers questions about the stock market. You type in some symbols and it outputs some other symbols on the screen; these are the stock prices for the day, let us say. What goes on inside the computer is that the program takes your symbols, compares them to what is in its memory bank, and outputs the symbols that have been programmed as the answer to the question. The computer just rearranges the symbols, giving out a sequence of symbols in response to an input of symbols. It has no idea what these symbols mean: what a stock is, what a price is, how your heart may lift or sink according to the symbols it so blindly displays. The symbols are interpreted by you and the programmer in a certain way, but the computer has no need to bother itself with meaning; it proceeds according to syntax alone. It is just as if I were to program you with a set of instructions on how to respond to sentences in a language you don't know. I say to you: "If you hear a sentence that sounds like this, 'Come sta?', then produce a sentence that sounds like this, 'Bene'." You could carry out this rule and have no idea what either sentence means, since you are just responding to one sound with another. The fact that the first sentence means "How are you?" in Italian and the second means "Fine" in the same language is of no concern to you, insofar as you are simply carrying out my program. The computer is like that: it associates symbols with symbols, without being concerned about what they mean. This is why computers work so well: they don't *have* to be programmed to respond to meaning, but only to shape. But the computer *appears* as if it knows what it is doing, because it has been cunningly programmed to manipulate symbols in a way that *mimics* understanding. Someone observing you respond with "Bene" to "Come sta?" would think you understood Italian, because you gave the appropriate response. But you do not understand Italian; you have simply been programmed to mimic understanding. And in principle you could be programmed this way with an indefinite number of Italian sentences, simply by getting you to remember many sentence-to-sentence pairings. You would be good at symbol manipulation, but you wouldn't thereby know any Italian.

Does this show that a robot could have a mind? Well, there
seems to be no difficulty with the idea that a robot could run
a computer program: we just have to install a sufficiently
complex syntactic algorithm in it. _If_ having a mind is running
a program, _then_ you have created a minded machine just by
inserting a program in it. If my understanding English is having a program in my head for manipulating sentences algo-
rithmically, then a machine could also understand English by
having a similar program inside it. The trouble is that this theory of mind is wrong as a matter of deep principle. Mental
processes are _not_ identifiable with symbol-manipulating algorithms. There are two big problems with the theory. The first
is that minds _do_ respond to meaning and not just to syntax.
When I respond to an English sentence with another one I do
so because I know what both sentences mean. I am not merely
parroting a rule for making one sound when I hear another
sound. I respond as I do _because_ of what the sentences mean.
My mental processes involve the manipulation of meanings,
not merely strings of syntax. I am a _semantic_ manipulator, as
well as a syntactic one. Understanding speech is pairing
meanings with sounds, not just producing one sound when
you hear another one, since that can be done without the as-
signment of meaning. And the point is that a computer carries
out its tasks without understanding the symbols it manipu-
lates. But then it can hardly aspire to duplicate (as opposed to
mimic) the operations of a mind that does essentially bring
understanding to its activities. A computer is a bit like an
actor: an actor behaves as if she has various beliefs and feel-

ings, as if she has this or that character, but she is only *acting*, that is, mimicking someone with those feelings and that character. An actor can put on a good show of being a great thinker or hero, but it is naive to suppose that she must be what she pretends to be. A computer likewise is playing a part, behaving as if it is something it is not. An actor can pretend to be a fearless action hero and not be one; a computer can pretend to understand sentences and yet not understand them. In both cases *acting* a certain way is not sufficient for *being* a certain way. Simulation is not replication. A computer can simulate the weather, after all, but that does not make it wet and windy inside.

What this tells us is that, while you may be able to build a machine that acts as if it has a mind by installing computer programs in it, you do not thereby build a machine that *really* has a mind. Running a program only mimics the grasp of meaning; it does not constitute grasp of meaning. If a machine is to think, therefore, then it must incorporate more than a syntactic algorithm. It needs a unit for manipulating meanings, a semantic processor. And this is something that the programs inside computing machines signally lack. Programs are semantically blind. That was the first point. The second point is that running a program does not guarantee sentience; in fact, it is neither necessary nor sufficient for sentience. It is not necessary because sentience in general does not involve symbolic manipulations. Consider the pains of a koala bear: these are states of consciousness, feelings, episodes of sentience, but they are not instances of symbol manipulation. A pain is no more a symbol than a heartbeat or a secretion of urine is. There is nothing *linguistic* about a koala in pain. And we are no different: our primitive sensations are not elements in a symbolic code, any more than our digestive juices are. So if you want to make a machine that has these kinds of sensations, there is no point in installing a whole lot of symbol manipulation. That would be like trying to build a machine with a bloodstream by equipping it with paper towels. I would say that sentience came on the evolutionary scene well before a symbol ever saw the light of day. Animals could feel before they could symbolize. In any case, a feeling is not the *same* as a symbol.

It is possible to run a computer program and have no consciousness at all. This should be obvious enough, since many machines today run programs but are not conscious by any stretch of the imagination. I like my computer, but I am not sentimental enough to believe that it harbors any feelings for me—or even for its computer buddies. It is no more conscious than the telephone, which also conveys symbols to me, in acoustic form. The computer, like the telephone, mediates between one conscious human mind and another, but it is a mindless intermediary in that process. The programmer has a mind, and that is evident in what the computer does; my interlocutor on the phone has a mind, and that is evident in what the phone does. But both are just unconscious machines designed to mediate between one conscious mind and another. The computer merely uses electronic pulses to rearrange its internal states; nothing in this implies that it is conscious. There is no more reason to believe a computer is conscious than to believe that a table is. A table also shows the mark of conscious agency behind it, since it was designed by a conscious mind. But it would be naive indeed to infer that tables themselves are conscious. In the same way, a computer is a human artifact in whose design considerable intelligence is evident, but that is no reason to credit *it* with consciousness. A computer is a high-tech puppet: you pull the strings and watch it respond, but it no more has a mind than Punch and Judy do. And making it more complex is not going to alter its basic character. If symbol manipulations do not produce consciousness in simpler cases, why should adding more of them make any difference? You do not eventually create cheese by multiplying pieces of chalk, so why should you be able to create consciousness by adding more symbol manipulations? Is a roomful of pocket calculators any nearer to consciousness than an isolated one? Could connecting them all together make any difference to their mindlessness?

What follows from all this is not that a robot could not be conscious. What follows is that a robot could not be conscious *in virtue* of being a computer—that is, in virtue of running computer programs. The property of running a program is the wrong property for bringing conscious minds into existence in the form of a machine. Such an idea is based on a bad theory of what consciousness is. But there might be other theories of consciousness that are better and that permit the possibility of conscious machines. If we could argue that consciousness is just internal combustion, say, then we would have a ready argument for the conclusion that machines can be conscious, namely, that cars run by internal combustion. The difficulty, really, is in coming up with a plausible theory of consciousness in the organic case. But before I pursue this thought further I want to discuss a very popular approach to the question of machine consciousness: the suggestion that a machine will count as conscious if and only if it passes what is called the Turing test.

## THE TURING TEST

When would we be justified in saying that a machine was conscious? The natural answer is that the machine would have to behave like a conscious being; if a machine behaves just like us, then it is reasonable to say that it is conscious like we are. The Turing test, named after Alan Turing, gives expression to this natural idea, but it stipulates a condition intended to prevent prejudice against counting a machine as conscious.[2] If you are confronted by a clanking robot, studded with flashing lights, serial numbers printed on it, rivets in its face, you will be apt to be prejudiced against it. You will be reluctant to count it a conscious being like yourself, no matter how impressively it behaves. But this is a form of discrimination based on appearance; you are a "flesh-and-bloodist," someone who irrationally reserves the label "conscious being" only for those of organic origin. To overcome this prejudice we need to exclude appearances from our judgments, and this is what the Turing test in effect does. The machine is put behind an opaque screen, or some equivalent, and you are allowed to communicate with it only by means of written messages; that way, you are not put off by its robotic appearance and inhuman voice. You then enter into a conversation with it on a topic of your choosing, asking it questions, receiving answers. If after a sufficient lapse of time the concealed robot behaves indistinguishably from a normal human interlocutor placed in the same conditions, then it is reasonable to declare it conscious. We have stripped the question down to its essentials, discounting irrelevant variables. If the machine gives the same evidence of mind in these conditions as a normal human would, then it would be mere prejudice to refuse to grant it consciousness. (I sometimes think this approach occurred to Alan Turing because of a prejudice to which he himself was subject, namely discrimination on the basis of sexual preference, Turing being a homosexual at a time when homosexual acts were illegal in Great Britain.) The essence of the Turing test is that <u>if a machine behaves like a normal human well enough to fool an unprejudiced observer, then it also should be considered conscious.</u> What its brain happens to be *made* of—whether indeed it has what we would call a brain—is irrelevant. What matters is that it *does* what conscious beings do. The Turing test "operationalizes" the question of machine consciousness by formulating it as a question about the activities of consciousness, not a question about its secret essence. <u>Consciousness is as consciousness does.</u>

The question of whether a conscious machine is possible is thus the question of whether a machine could pass the Turing test. And this seems to brighten the prospects for machine consciousness, since there is no obvious reason why we could not make a machine that behaves as we behave; we just need to rig it up so that it mimics the physical processes that underlie our own behavior. In other words, we need a machine simulation of the activities of the brain, which is itself a physical object. If we can make a machine that has internal physical states that control its verbal outputs as our verbal outputs are controlled by our brain, then we will have made a conscious machine. Of course, this may be fiendishly difficult to do and well beyond our current technology, but it doesn't sound out of the question. Machines can already mimic many of the things we do, so why can they not mimic even more? It doesn't matter *how* the machine contrives to mimic us—what is going on inside its chambers and circuits—as long as it passes the Turing test. After all, we judge other people to be conscious on the basis of behavior without bothering to delve into their interior workings, so we should extend the same courtesy to the aspiring robot. What matters is performance, not what color you are on the inside.

However, egalitarian as the Turing test may seem, I think it gives a poor criterion for machine consciousness. There are two problems with it. In the first place, it does not provide a *necessary* condition for consciousness, since many conscious beings would fail the Turing test miserably. If you put a cat behind the curtain and start in with your probing questions, you will not get much of a response. The odd *miaow* may appear on the screen in front of you as you inquire into your interlocutor's views on foreign policy and the national debt, but mostly you will be met with a deafening silence. Cats don't speak, but they are conscious: they see and smell, feel pain, have their cat urges. And so it is with the legions of other speechlessly conscious organisms that populate the planet. This suggests that the Turing test is not focusing on what is essential to consciousness: the possession of what-it's-likeness, simple sentience. Human prelinguistic children will be declared mindless by the Turing test, yet they are bursting with sensations and feelings of many types. The test is too linguistically oriented.

The second problem is that the criterion is not sufficient either. The trouble is that the Turing test is either committed to a behaviorist analysis of consciousness or it is logically insufficient for consciousness. If we really could analyze our own consciousness in behavioral terms, so that being conscious just consisted of behaving in a certain way, then indeed behaving in that way would be sufficient for consciousness—in animals or machines. But such an analysis is hopelessly wide of the mark. Conscious states *cause* behavior, they are not *reducible* to behavior. Having a sensation of pain is not the same thing as your body moving in a certain way as a response to a stimulus. You could be in pain and suppress the response, or you could move that way and only be pretending to be in pain. Behaviorism is just another version of the kind of materialism we have already rejected. Of course, it is quite true that behavior gives us a reason to suppose that there are conscious states causing it, but this is an inference from one thing to another, not a simple deduction based on identity. And the behavioral evidence is always fallible: something can behave as if it is conscious and yet not be. An actor can act as if he is in pain but not be. A seducer can feign love for his own nefarious purposes. A malingerer can pretend to be asleep when she is actually wide awake. Behavior gives evidence for consciousness, but it does not guarantee consciousness.

Because of this logical gap it is in principle possible for a machine to behave as if it is conscious and not be. Maybe the manufacturer of a machine that passes the Turing test has simply made something that acts *as if* it is conscious while not being so. She has made a robot that produces the right outputs, but that is all; there is still no consciousness in there. This is a point that came up in the previous section: there is a distinction between simulating a mind and having a mind. The Turing test tries to say when a machine would be conscious without giving any *theory* of what consciousness *is*. It merely tells us when it would be reasonable to ascribe consciousness to an entity. But it can be reasonable to ascribe consciousness to something even if it is *false* that that thing is conscious. You can have evidence for something's being the case even when it is not in fact the case. If I come upon you holding a smoking gun over a recently deceased individual, I have a reason to suppose that you did the murder. But you might nevertheless not be the real murderer; it merely looks as if you are. It is thus entirely conceivable that we could build a machine that passes the Turing test with flying colors and yet there might not be even a flicker of consciousness in the damn thing. We might never come to know that this is the true situation, but it could still *be* so.

To be sure that we have a conscious machine on our hands, we need to know what consciousness *is;* we can then check to see whether our machine has *that.* Merely knowing that it acts as if it were conscious does not settle the question. Even if it could be proved right now that we can make a behavioral analogue of a conscious being from paper and sealing wax in a few hours ("some assembly required"), that would not settle whether we had really made a conscious being. For there might be more than one way to engineer an entity with this behavioral description, with consciousness or without. The behavior by itself does not tell us which of these we have before us.

The upshot of this discussion is that neither the computer model of mind nor the Turing test is adequate to decide whether machine consciousness is in principle possible. In fact, if we put these two ideas together, we can see that the Turing test *must* be inadequate, given what we said earlier about the computational theory of mind. The point about programs is that they *can* mimic intelligent mental processes; that is, they can give rise to outputs that simulate thinking. This means that we can program a machine to perform a task without thinking that we solve by means of thinking. The great discovery about computers is that not all cognitive tasks require intelligence to perform. That is why calculating machines are possible: they do without mind and intelligence what we do with mind and intelligence. We could even agree that *any* cognitive task that we carry out by means of intelligence, understanding, and consciousness *could* be carried out purely mechanically, without those faculties, just by means of a series of electronically realized algorithmic steps. Any piece of rational mental activity would thus have a computational *counterpart*. The counterpart achieves nonmentally what we achieve mentally. But then it *follows* that a machine could pass the Turing test and have no mind, because it could simulate what we do with our minds with a program that is entirely mind-free. If we can in principle do X without having Y, then the fact that we can do X does not prove that we have Y. If algorithms are as powerful as human reasoning, then they could pass the Turing test. But this shows that passing the Turing test is no proof of mentality. So it is not merely conceptually possible for something to pass the Turing test and not be conscious. We also have good reason to believe that this is a real theoretical possibility in view of the demonstrated power of computational systems. If a computer can play chess at grandmaster level, it can pass the Turing test with respect to the game of chess. But it does so without a glimmer of consciousness inside it, just a set of very powerful (but mindless) algorithms.

## WHAT IS A MACHINE?

We have still not arrived at an answer to the question of whether a machine could be conscious. All we know is that this cannot be so in virtue of embodying computations or passing the Turing test. Perhaps it will help if we step back for a moment and examine our terms; maybe we are not formulating the issue precisely enough.[3] What is meant by "machine" anyway? In one use of the term it means the same as "artifact," that is, a product of intelligent design intentionally created. Tables and televisions and tractors are artifacts. So, could there be a conscious artifact? The answer must surely be yes. If the creationist story of human origins is true, then we conscious beings *are* all artifacts, since we are the result of God's intentional actions as a designer and builder of the world. That story is not true, of course, but if it were it would hardly preclude us from being conscious. So long as an artifact is constructed so as to be internally indistinguishable from a conscious organism, it must also be conscious. If I were to discover tomorrow that I was created by Martians and put here among naturally evolved humans for some strange Martian purpose, I would not conclude that I am not conscious after all. Being intentionally created does not disqualify one from being conscious. If we reach the point where we can make a brain just like a naturally evolved brain from a few pounds of basic raw materials, then we will have made a conscious being, and the origins of that brain will not matter one way or the other. Consciousness is not an origin-dependent property like being a Ford motor car or a Leonardo da Vinci painting. It is an intrinsic property of whatever contains it. So there is no problem of principle about conscious artifacts, however rare or nonexistent they may actually be.

Maybe we can formulate something a bit more interesting by changing our definition of "machine." Suppose we mean by "machine" a "physical object obeying physical laws." Then our question is whether there can be a physical object obeying physical laws that is conscious. The answer to this question is also pretty clearly yes, because the body and brain are machines in this sense, and they are conscious. The body and brain are physical objects obeying physical laws (as well as chemical, biological, and psychological laws), and together they form a person with consciousness. So, yes, machines in this sense can be conscious, whether naturally evolved or artifacts. That is not to say that brains are conscious *in virtue of* such physical properties and laws: no doubt they are not, as we have argued earlier. That brains are subject to the laws of motion, to relativistic time dilation and length contraction, just like any other physical object, is not the reason for their *also* being the basis of consciousness. Brains must have additional properties that distinguish them from the general run of insentient projectiles subject to gravity and other forces. All we have said is that a conscious entity could have machine-like properties in addition to its being conscious; we have not said that consciousness is itself a machine-like property. I am a conscious machine, after all, because I am both conscious and have a body subject to the laws and forces of physics. My nature is to be a center of consciousness embodied in a machine. That is the glory of mortal life as well as its tragedy, for machines break down, cease to function, grind to a sickening halt. Can a machine be conscious? Yes, thank God, because otherwise we would never exist in the form in which we do, imperfect and breakable as we are. We are often exhorted to acknowledge our "animal nature"; just as important is the recognition that we have the frailties and limits of all machines. There may or may not be a ghost in the machine, but there is certainly a machine whose mechanical functioning is of the deepest concern to our consciousness.

We seem to be defining the word "machine" so that conscious machines can exist rather easily. Can we be more restrictive? Well, in one use of the term a machine is defined simply as something that is *not* conscious. "A worm has no mind, it is just a machine." "His actions were completely mechanical, not the result of thinking at all." "I am a man, not a machine." Using the term this way, obviously machines cannot be conscious by definition. We are using the word in such a way that we presuppose that "machine" and "conscious" cannot apply to the same thing. That is not at all interesting; it merely reflects a determination to use the word in a certain way. No substantive issue is thereby joined. Nevertheless, I sometimes detect a tendency to trivialize the issue in this way, through inattention to the use of terms.

Perhaps at least one of the things that is meant by the question of machine consciousness turns essentially upon a contrast between the organic and the inorganic. We know that organic machines can be conscious; we just have to feel the throbbing of our own consciousness and note its mechanical shell. And there are millions more like us on the planet. But none of this vast ocean of consciousness ever seems to emanate from an inorganic source. Is this just an accident, or is it somehow essential to consciousness that it spring from organic roots? Does consciousness necessarily result from biological tissue? Must a conscious being be a meat head? It is notable that the creatures of fantasy who most clearly exhibit consciousness are always at least partly organic, however machine-like their speech, movements, and manners are apt to be. Consider the Borg from *Star Trek Voyager*, whose most prominent representative is the redoubtable Seven of Nine: these are creatures made originally of organic tissue but thoroughly supplemented with inorganic implants, even down to the cellular level. Then there is Robocop, the mostly mechanical remnant of a flesh-and-blood human. These hybrids come equipped with inorganic components joined to human flesh. In the case of Robocop, only the human face peeps out from behind a carapace of hi-tech metal, while in the case of Seven of Nine far more of her human form is visible (devotees of the show will know what I mean). These beings are stiff and unsmiling, partly wedded to their mechanical selves, but we are left in no doubt of their inner consciousness—compromised, indeed, but still pressing, still vivid. So a *partly* inorganic entity can be conscious. But how much? We are not told, but the suggestion is that it is a human brain that squats behind those robotic eyes. And if this is an accurate depiction of theoretical possibility, then one way to build a conscious machine is to put an organic brain into an inorganic body.

## INORGANIC BRAINS

Now we reach the central issue: Could an inorganic *brain* be conscious? Could you make a conscious brain out of inorganic materials? Could it be made of silicon chips, say, or laser beams, or beer cans? Or will only squishy neurons do? I think the answer to this question ought to be the result of strict agnosticism combined with commonsense skepticism. My whole point so far has been that we do not know the solution to the mind-body problem. We know we have minds and we know that brains arc somehow responsible for them, but we do not know what it is about brains that brings consciousness into existence. The mechanism of consciousness is a mystery. But then how are we to *say* whether an inorganic brain could be conscious? If we knew what made *our* brain conscious, then we could ask whether that property could exist in an inorganic system. But we are in the dark on the question simply because we don't know what makes our brains conscious. Some properties of the brain could be duplicated in a machine brain—its size, weight, color, electrical activity; others could not—the biochemistry of cell growth, the flow of blood, the hormones. Into which category does consciousness fall? Call the property that would explain consciousness, if only we knew it C*: is C* possible in inorganic materials or not? We cannot really say, because we don't know kind of property C* *is*. We must remain strictly agnostic on the question. To resolve the issue of machine minds we would need to solve the problem of meat minds, the problem of how *organic* brains are conscious. According to my theory of mysterianism, however, that question is not answerable by the human intellect. It follows that the question of the existence of inorganic brains is also strictly unanswerable. We might be able to make machines that behave like conscious beings, thus establishing that an outward simulation of consciousness is possible, but that would not necessarily be the same as making machines that really have consciousness. We might even accidentally make a machine with a mind, like accidentally making gunpowder. But unless we know what constitutes the very essence of consciousness, we will not be able to assert definitively that our machine is conscious.

Here the issue intersects with the old problem of other minds. Notoriously, we cannot know for sure that there are minds other than our own. I know that my consciousness exists in the most direct way possible, but my reason for thinking that you have consciousness is not direct in this way; it is based on indirect evidence. While it is not conceivable to me that my consciousness does not exist, it is conceivable to me that yours may not: you might just be a mindless robot for all that I can know. To settle the question of other minds definitively I need to know what makes my consciousness exist in me. For if I knew what property of my brain was the necessary and sufficient basis for my consciousness, then I could check to see whether your brain has that property too. If it does, then you are conscious also; if not, then not (sorry, pal). But without this kind of knowledge the problem of the existence of other minds will always exist, tantalizing us with the possibility that we are the only ones burdened with consciousness. I may indeed be right in my customary assumption that you have a mind like me, but I don't know *why* I am right. To solve the problem of other minds, in other words, we need to solve the mind-body problem. The problems are not separable. So if we ask "Do other people have minds?" we must take the same strictly agnostic position I am recommending for the question "Could a machine be conscious?" It all depends on what *makes* something have a conscious mind, and we don't know what that is. Only knowledge of this would enable us to say categorically whether other brains, organic *or* inorganic, house minds. In the absence of this knowledge I can only be sure that *I* have consciousness. And the reason for that is that I can be sure I have consciousness *without* solving the mind-body problem, because of the unique access I have to my own consciousness. If it were not that I had such access, then I would not be in a position to state conclusively that *anything* was conscious.

Now all this has been at a high theoretical or philosophical level; I have been talking about knowledge of a strong skepticism-proof kind. But that is consistent with supposing that we might have commonsense reasons for believing in other minds, as well as that only organic brains could be conscious. Maybe we cannot *definitively* answer these questions, but we might be able to find reasons for favoring one view over the other, however tentatively. Is it then more *likely* that other people have minds than that they do not? And is it more *likely* that brains have to be organic to produce minds than that they do not? I think the answer to both questions is yes. It is likely that others have minds because they are similar to me behaviorally and physiologically, so it would be anomalous if they were not similar in the further respect of having a mind like me. They certainly give a strong *impression* of having minds. Similarly, it is reasonable to assume that there is a strong connection between consciousness and organic tissue for the simple reason that there are no actual exceptions to this rule. All the cases of consciousness we know of are associated with organic brains. Induction therefore suggests that this assumption is backed by some kind of necessary truth. It would be different if certain complex crystals exhibited signs of consciousness, having little crystalline eyes and ears and ways of behaving. Then we would have empirical reason to believe that we could build an inorganic machine with consciousness. But in actual fact all the known cases of consciousness are organic in nature, so it is reasonable to suppose that organic tissue is necessary, although in ways we do not comprehend. I say "reasonable," not "infallible," because *maybe* it is just an accident that all minds are organically based, a consequence of technological backwardness on our part. After all, at one time the only pumps that existed were organic, namely, animal hearts. But now there are many kinds of inorganic pumps in the world, built by us. It turns out that a pumping system can be constructed out of many kinds of materials, not just organic tissue. The case of consciousness *might* be like that. We are simply not in a position to be sure. A gambling man might bet one way or the other, but he would be operating in a theoretical vacuum. Still, I think it is a fair bet, given what we observe, that consciousness needs an organic basis, although I would not be amazed if this turned out to be incorrect.

It follows that all the heated debate about machine minds is based on nothing solid. It is just so much ungrounded opinion. Once we are quite clear about the issue we can see that it can be resolved only by possessing a piece of knowledge we do not (and probably cannot) possess. That is, presumably, why the argument tends to be so heated and ideologically motivated. It is wiser to stand back and remain skeptical on the issue. Some people say that we can never know one way or the other whether God exists; this kind of knowledge transcends what we can expect to aspire to. Whether or not that is the case, I am saying that we cannot know for sure one way or the other whether machine consciousness is possible, in the sense of inorganically based consciousness. Meat-based consciousness might be the only possible kind, or it might be just one instance of many possible kinds of physical basis for consciousness.

## SMART ZOMBIES

I want to mention one other question before leaving this topic. We have been dissecting the question of whether a machine could be conscious, but what about the question of what a machine could do *without* being conscious? Could a machine do what we do and have no genuine mentality in it? Could a machine simulate the behavior of a cat or a kangaroo and have no conscious states? In other words, how necessary is consciousness to behaving as we or other animals do? Certainly an unconscious system can do *some* of the things

sentient animals do, but how much? Here again I think res-
olute skepticism is the only rational answer. We just don't
know how much difference consciousness makes to the behavior of a system that has it. We don't know how necessary
consciousness is to performing certain specific functions.
Could humanlike speech be produced by an unconscious system? Could there be intelligent planning by an organism that
was never conscious—all of whose planning went on in its
unconscious mind? Does creativity require consciousness?
The underlying question here is whether consciousness *adds*
anything in the organization of mental function. Could we get
on without it? On the face of it, the functions that animals
carry out consciously they could just as well carry out uncon-
sciously, so why do they bother to be conscious? The question
can be formulated in terms of evolution: Why does evolution
produce animals with consciousness instead of just mindless
zombies? In what way is consciousness essential to perpetuating the genes? It appears as if the genes *think* it is essential because they produce it with such regularity, but it is hard to
see *why* it is so necessary. Is there perhaps another planet in
the universe on which life has evolved and consciousness has
not come into the picture at all? I don't mean primitive life,
but intelligent technological life. Is it just an accident that our
planet has evolved consciousness, or is it indispensable to generating creatures with the behavioral capacities to live on
Earth? Might we have evolved to be essentially what we are
today, but without any consciousness, just a species of zombies with the same degree of civilization and technology we

have today? It is a contingent fact that we are usually born with ten fingers and without blue hair: Is our consciousness similarly contingent?

I don't think we can answer this last question in our current state of knowledge, because we don't understand what difference consciousness makes to animal life. But it is certainly a fascinating and unnerving question. What if it turns out that all the other life-forms in the universe are unconscious robots, albeit many of them vastly superior to us in technology, peacefulness, family values, and so on? We may not be alone, but we might not much enjoy the company of these mindless beings. Or is it that we will never come to know that they are unconscious, given that they behave so much like us? I would *like* to think that we can only engineer complex behavior by installing consciousness, but I see no good argument for assuming this. Maybe it is sheer luck that we are conscious; we were just one mutation away from perpetual mindlessness. Maybe our distant ancestors evolved consciousness by sheer chance, as one among many options. Maybe there is no evolutionary inevitability about consciousness at all. On a good day that sounds like a near tragedy; on a bad day it doesn't sound so terrible. Consciousness is the joy and bane of life, but whether it is necessary for life—even life as complex as ours—is an open question.

# 7

# The Unbearable Heaviness of Philosophy

## Philosophy and Science

The mind-body problem is a problem in philosophy. This means that it generates a peculiar kind of conceptual bafflement. It belongs to a set of problems that have perplexed the human intellect for centuries. In this book I have argued that the difficulty of the problem reflects our cognitive limitations. This suggests that the subject we call "philosophy" might in general be characterized by cognitive closure problems. In this final chapter I take a step back and locate the problem of consciousness within the general class of philosophical problems, so that we can appreciate its place on the map of human knowledge. That map has its high points and low points, and it is predictable on general grounds that human knowledge should be thus configured. The problems of philosophy, of which the mind-body problem is a notable instance, arise from problems *in* philosophy: problems in achieving this very kind of knowledge. After I have surveyed these problems with philosophy itself I can go on to consider what might be done to remedy our present intellectual frailties.

Philosophy is defined in the dictionary as the search for knowledge, especially of ultimate reality and of the general principles of things. Philosophers seek understanding of the world in its deepest recesses and most puzzling corners, striving to remedy our ignorance of the world in which we live, and to relieve the perplexities to which the world gives rise. Such an elevated quest is not easy to accomplish. And there is no guarantee that it will succeed. Philosophy attempts to get beyond the confines of our individual minds, with their personal histories and idiosyncrasies, to grasp how reality is in itself, right down to its ultimate principles. Philosophy wants to bring the world up close and gaze into its inner constitution, so that everything falls into place under the bright light of universal reason. It wants the world to lie completely open before its all-seeing eyes. This is nothing if not an ambitious enterprise, not to say an audacious one. No wonder it was deemed impious in a bygone age.

This definition of philosophy makes no distinction between different branches of knowledge, except to emphasize its concern with what is general and ultimate. No distinction is drawn between physics, astronomy, and biology, on the one hand, and the speculative study of the mind, on the other. The quantum theorist is as much of a philosopher, under this definition, as the student of the mind-body problem. Both types of theorist can be described as "natural philosophers," as distinct from ethical and political theorists, who are customarily described as "moral philosophers." The natural philosopher is concerned about understanding the deepest principles of the natural world, including matter and consciousness, while the moral philosopher is interested in determining how things ought to be, individually or socially. The student of cosmology is concerned to understand how the universe came to be and the laws that govern its evolution; the student of consciousness likewise wants to understand how consciousness originates and what the laws of its operation are. Both seek knowledge of how the world works in its large-scale features.

From the dawning of systematic knowledge at the time of the ancient Greeks two thousand years ago, up to the scientific revolution of the seventeenth century and beyond, it was customary to use the word "philosophy" in this broad, undiscriminating manner. We were all seekers after the truth of the world. But in the last hundred years or so this way of carving up the intellectual landscape has undergone a marked change. We now speak of "scientists" versus "philosophers," as if a sharp dichotomy existed. Scientists have laboratories, go on field trips, crunch numbers, verify each other's results; philosophers sit in their offices (or at home) and rack their brains to relieve their perplexities, occasionally meeting with each other to have a good long argument. Scientists make observations, invent theories, test them, communicate their results, reach a consensus. But what do philosophers do? They make no observations, test no theories, communicate no results; instead, they argue with their colleagues, and scarcely ever reach consensus.

Philosophy is not the same as science. Science asks answerable questions and moves steadily forward, eliminating false theories, reducing the area of human ignorance, while philosophy seems mired in controversy, perpetually worrying at the same questions, not making the kind of progress characteristic of science. Why is this? It can hardly be that scientists are just much smarter than philosophers, outshining them in sheer IQ. There are, and always have been, plenty of highly intelligent people in philosophy,  some of them well trained in science. And it is not as if when a scientist makes a foray into philosophy he or she outshines the resident professionals; on the contrary, the results are often laughably bad. No, the difference has something to do with the nature of the *subject,* with the questions themselves and the methods available for answering them. Philosophy is *hard*. Milan Kundera wrote a novel called *The Unbearable Lightness of Being,* which can be contrasted with the "Unbearable Heaviness of Thinking about Being." I speak as one who knows; I have spent most of my adult life feeling the burden of this heaviness.[1]

The difficulty of philosophy has often been attributed to its asking "fake" questions. Science asks meaningful questions with answers we can in principle discover, but philosophy (it is said) indulges in meaningless pseudo-questions that cannot be rationally answered. At best it is poetry dressed up as science; at worst it is so much pretentious gibberish. This is an understandable response to what seems an undeniable fact: that philosophy is intellectually static compared to science. Philosophy does indeed lack the kind of systematic scientific method characteristic of physics, astronomy, and biology. But I think the idea that philosophical questions are meaningless pseudo-questions is an exaggerated and implausible response to that fact. The question of the relation between mind and body is a perfectly meaningful question, however hard it may be to answer it. Consciousness is a real phenomenon with a real nature, somehow linked to the nature of matter. Discussion about the problematic link between consciousness and the brain is by no means gibberish. But then what does explain the static nature of philosophy? Why do its problems seem so intractable? Why do philosophical questions make the head spin?

## A BRIEF HISTORY OF THOUGHT

The answer towards which this book has tended is this: philosophy marks the limit of human theoretical intelligence. Philosophy is an attempt to overstep our cognitive bounds, a kind of magnificent failure. Let me retell the history of human thought with this idea in mind. My aim is to be schematic, not detailed; I want to bring out the broad shape of intellectual history. And I want to approach intellectual history in a naturalistic spirit, viewing it as a part of the natural history of human beings.

We can imagine our hunter-gatherer ancestors going about their quotidian business some ten thousand years ago, not bothering themselves too much about the deep problems of natural philosophy. There was no agriculture then, nothing in the way of cities, very primitive politics, no books, no schools or universities. The problems of science and philosophy had probably not even been formulated at this time. Nevertheless, the brains of these unsophisticated forebears were not significantly different from ours in their basic biological structure. They had the potential to create science and philosophy, unlike the brains of rabbits and crocodiles, but actually doing so lay in the far distant future. Maybe they entertained some primitive religious ideas, a heavy dose of animism, an abundance of superstition. Then the first reflective Greeks came along, no doubt assisted by the Egyptians and others. These people were the first great theorists of nature, with their earth, fire, and water, their anthropocentric cosmology. After the shaky but impressive start of the pre-Socratics, the ancient Greeks got into their stride, and soon the world had Plato, Euclid, Pythagoras, Aristotle, Archimedes, Aristarchus, and many others. Almost miraculously these thinkers inaugurated the scientific age, formulating the questions that were to preoccupy thinkers to this day. The ideal of objective knowledge was invented. Superstition and irrationalism were given their marching orders. The study of "philosophy" in the broadest sense was set in motion.[2]

There then followed the dark medieval period, in which the insights of the Greeks were all but forgotten. Science and philosophy languished. Rational knowledge of nature was set back. Then, finally, came the miraculous outburst of the Renaissance—Copernicus, Kepler, Galileo, Newton, Descartes, Boyle—the founders of the modern scientific world-view.

Physics and astronomy were set on a solid course, mathematics flourished, nature began to yield up its secrets to the inquiring mind. The scientific method triumphed: Observation combined with systematic theoretical construction became the way to discover what the world is all about. Within a few hundred years Darwin made the big breakthrough in biology, the theory of evolution by natural selection. The world of objects in motion, chemical substances, and living things began to seem transparent to human understanding, susceptible of scientific explanation. On this sure basis human knowledge then expanded dramatically, with physics, chemistry, astronomy, and biology all achieving remarkable successes. Our Greek ancestors—not to mention their hunter-gatherer forebears—would be amazed and thrilled at the extent and depth of human knowledge. The wildest hopes of the early philosophers had been amply fulfilled. The world began to seem like a place to which the human intellect is naturally tuned, instead of being intrinsically recalcitrant to our efforts at understanding. We started to seem like a species set apart from others, the thinking species, the born knowers, the natural omniscients. True, it takes some effort and many years for a human individual to master the principles of nature that have been discovered, but the human mind seems perfectly cut out for the job. There seems no reason to believe that the age of understanding will ever come to an end. Everything will eventually disclose its secrets to our cognitive probings.

But there is a dark side to this story of human achievement, a sort of embarrassment, like the retarded relative in the back room. One area of human inquiry constitutes an anomaly, a black spot into which the light of reason seems not able to penetrate: the subject we now call "philosophy." The classic problems of philosophy have not yielded to this forward rush of cognitive expansion. The mind-body problem, in particular, stubbornly resists our efforts to resolve it. Here the human intellect stumbles. The thesis I have been defending in this book is that this failure of understanding results from the structure of human intelligence. The question of the relationship of mind and body is perfectly genuine, but our minds are not equipped to solve it, rather as the cat's mind is not up to discovering relativity theory or evolution by natural selection. I suggest that the history of human inquiry, with its areas of success and failure, is confirmation of this thesis. What we have in effect discovered over the centuries is that certain problems lie within the scope of our cognitive faculties, while others do not. The contemporary demarcation between science and philosophy is really a reflection of this differential intellectual aptitude. In short, what we call "philosophy" is a scientific problem we are constitutionally unequipped to solve. The Greeks were right to sense a homogeneity across the field of "natural philosophy," but it was not until after the Renaissance that we discovered that this homogeneity in the type of question being asked does not lead to uniform solvability. The mind-body problem is the same *kind* of problem as the problems of physics and other sciences; we just lack the conceptual equipment with which to solve it. The history of human thought is thus a kind of map of the human cognitive system, revealing its strengths and weaknesses.

We can imagine that this map could have been different. Consider a hypothetical intellectual history for beings from another galaxy, and imagine that the constraints on mental evolution are different there. These alien beings invert our intellectual history. Their "ancient Greeks" initiated systematic thought, treating all their questions as of a piece. But in their case the problems of physics, astronomy, and biology turned out to be the recalcitrant questions, given their specific mental make-up. What we call philosophical problems they have a knack for answering; solving the mind-body problem is one of their early triumphs, now taught in their version of kindergarten to all normal children. But they cannot for the life of them fathom the laws of motion, and they *still* believe their planet is the center of the universe. They are very bad at understanding matter in space, but they are excellent at understanding the nature of the mind. That is just the way their brains evolved. Such an inverted intellectual history seems quite conceivable, and I think the natural explanation for it would be along the lines I am suggesting: their cognitive architecture is biased in favor of problems of mind and away from problems of matter. Reflecting on the history of their own knowledge, they would naturally come to this conclusion. I would certainly urge this view on them, should they ever pay us a visit (unlikely, given their ineptitude with physics).

The hardness and heaviness of philosophy is thus a reflection of our cognitive biases, rather as the difficulty of flying unaided reflects our motor biases (no wings, you see). Our hands and arms are good for picking things up and manipulating them, but are poor organs for flying with. Our cognitive faculties are good for solving physics problems, but weak when it comes to problems of mind. It is not that we have not *tried* hard enough with philosophy, or that we insist on posing pseudo-questions to ourselves, or that philosophy deals with an especially elevated region of reality. It is just that our brains are not cut out to handle questions of this class. Speaking loftily, it is just a matter of bad cognitive *luck* that we cannot solve the mind-body problem; our minds happen not to have been engineered that way. According to this view of philosophy, then, the mind-body problem is a symptom of a more general cognitive weakness: it reflects a systematic fault-line in our ability to understand the world. Philosophy in general poses similar problems of cognitive limitation.

## THE FORM OF THE SOLUTION

Does this mean we can say nothing about consciousness and what a solution to the mind-body problem would look like? Not at all. We can still describe the contents of consciousness, and we can investigate how these contents vary from the underlying neurophysiology. We can still "do" the psychology of consciousness, conceived as the study of the role of consciousness in mental functioning. Nothing I have said puts paid to the scientific research programs currently dedicated to unraveling the neural correlates of different conscious states. All I have said is that the *philosophical* mind-body problem cannot be solved: the problem of explaining how brains can give rise to consciousness in the first place. Moreover, we can know quite a bit about the *form* a solution to the mind-body problem would have to take. As I argued earlier, it is plausible to suppose that such a solution would have to detail the hidden structure of consciousness itself (chapter 5) and that it would call for a revision in our view of the nature of space (chapter 4).

The solution would also, I think, have to take the form of a statement of what consciousness *is*, and that statement would have to be *conceptually* necessary. This idea is a little technical, but let me try to explain the gist of it. What I mean is that, first, the solution would have to go beyond merely saying what consciousness is correlated with and tell us about the very essence of consciousness; and, second, it would have to do so in such a way that we could see how consciousness could arise from the brain with the force of conceptual necessity. It would have to be as obvious that consciousness could arise from the brain as it is obvious that bachelors are unmarried males. That last proposition states an analytic or conceptual connection between the concept *bachelor* and the concept *unmarried male*. I am saying that if the mind-body problem is to be solved, something like this kind of conceptual connection has to exist between mental concepts and concepts of the brain. The very concept of consciousness has to be connected to concepts of the brain in an internal way.

Only then would we have an intelligible explanation of the nature of the link.

This last point implies that our current concepts of consciousness are inadequate to figure in the true explanation of consciousness. There simply is no conceptual connection between our current mental concepts and any concepts of the brain. You can know that you are in pain and not know anything about what is going on in your brain, so there is no conceptual link between the concept of pain that you have and any concepts of the brain. But there has to be such a link with *some* possible concept of pain. Let us suppose that the concept in question is expressed by a new word, "PAIN," where the concept expressed does connect analytically with certain brain concepts. Then we can say that the solution to the mind-body problem has the form "PAIN is identical to brain state #," where brain state # is the brain state that actually explains pain and "PAIN" expresses a concept that connects to the concept expressed by "brain state #" in an internal and necessary way. Less cumbersomely, "PAIN" gives us a new way of thinking of pain (the thing itself) that enables us to appreciate how pain arises from the underlying brain state. The new concept provides us with a way to understand how pain sensations can arise from brain processes. We thus need two new concepts to formulate the solution, one for the mind and one for the brain. That is, radical conceptual innovation is a necessary prerequisite for solving the mind-body problem.

It is not that we can now go on to acquire these concepts; my entire argument has been that they are beyond us. But we can at least know that they have to exist. We can know, that is, that radically new concepts are necessary and that they would have to be connected to each other rather in the way that "bachelor" is connected to "unmarried male." In sum, the form of the solution to the mind-body problem must be a conceptually true statement involving radically new concepts that reveal the deep structure of consciousness and that call for a new conception of the nature of space. If I am right, we are not going to come up with that solution. But we do at least know something about what it would look like in its general form. All is not darkness. When Einstein figured out that an adequate new physics would have to accommodate the constant speed of light, he was certainly onto something extremely important, but that was not yet to produce the theory that actually does accommodate that remarkable fact. He knew that the earlier Newtonian theory had to be wrong in view of the constancy of the speed of light, and he knew that only radical revisions would explain this, calling for a quite new conception of the nature of motion, but the actual principles of relativity theory took a lot more working out. And there was no guarantee that he or anyone else *would* work them out. Luckily, the new principles were not outside the scope of human intelligence, although several strokes of genius were required for their discovery. I am saying that we are in a somewhat similar position with respect to the mind-body problem. We know that the current theories are inadequate, and we know that the correct solution will have to change our view of space and credit consciousness with a hidden dimension, but we are not in a position to produce the theory that will satisfy these conditions. Nor will we ever be, if the cognitive closure thesis is correct. We can see where the theoretical lack lies, which is a kind of insight, but whether the lack can be filled is another question, which I answer negatively.

## New Brains for Old

Is there any way forward from here? Not if we have only our current cognitive faculties to go on. But possibly we can acquire *new* faculties. Let us speculate about this possibility for a while; if nothing else, it will help in understanding the nature of the claim I am making. The human brain has changed its make-up quite substantially in the last few hundred thousand years. The frontal lobes, in particular, those factories of intellection, have grown much larger than they were in our prehuman ancestors (the "missing links"). Accordingly, human intelligence has changed considerably, as a function of these cortical enhancements. Science and philosophy have been one notable result of this development. Moreover, the brain is an organ in the process of construction, not a fixed quantity for all time. How might it change further in the future? We can expect that natural selection will continue to do its work, resulting in long term-changes to brain structure and function. But there is no guarantee that these changes will result in greater theoretical intelligence; they may even turn out to be retrograde in this respect. Already the size of a human baby's head poses problems of transition from womb to world, for both baby and mother. How much bigger can it get? And are capacities for theoretical intelligence the kinds of capacities that the genes *want* to promulgate? Theoretical intelligence is apt to go with an unworldly disposition, not a propensity to maximize one's progeny. Why spend years on child rearing if your main interest is cosmology and the nature of consciousness? Maybe our frontal lobes will shrink over the next million years, and interest in natural philosophy will fade away. So we certainly cannot rely on *natural* selection to fashion brains that are apt for solving philosophical problems.

But there is always the possibility of *artificial* selection. Can this be used to manufacture more intellectually effective brains? There are two routes that might be taken here: selective breeding and direct genetic engineering. Let me hasten to say that I am not *advocating* these methods; there are clearly all sorts of ethical problems that would arise from such a project. My interest is purely theoretical, to understand what it would be to be able to solve the mind-body problem. In principle, then, we might breed thinkers as we breed dogs, to be specialized in certain kinds of tasks. The innate structure of the canine brain is affected by selective breeding; so too might the brains of human beings be bred to solve philosophical problems. But this method is quite slow and cumbersome; it might be more effective to operate directly on the genes. Some of our genes are responsible for determining the make-up of the human brain, so it seems within the bounds of possibility that we might be able to engineer the DNA in such a way as to change the kind of brain possessed by a subject.

Suppose a gene, "G," has the job of determining the density of neurons in the frontal lobes. (I am simplifying tremendously to make a conceptual point.) Then we might manipulate "G" to increase the density of such neurons, thus enhancing the cognitive power of the frontal lobes, where reasoning is primarily located. Or we might enhance the language centers in the left hemisphere of the brain by such genetic intervention. Who knows what this might do for the problem-solving powers of the person whose souped up brain this is? But probably the areas to focus on are the brain centers that subserve the faculty of introspection. Suppose that consciousness possesses a hidden structure not open to introspective access. Suppose also that this hidden structure contains the solution to the mind-body problem. Then enhancing the scope of introspective awareness might be just what is needed to solve the problem, or at least to provide crucial data for a solution. Presumably the introspective faculty has a basis in the brain that is ultimately determined by the genetic program of human beings; that is, we have a gene for inspecting consciousness introspectively. If so, then it ought to be possible in principle to manipulate this gene in ways that might enlarge the scope of that faculty. This is pure science fiction, of course, at our current stage of genetic engineering, but I am interested only in raising a theoretical possibility, so that we can see what might be involved in producing a mind that can perform better than ours at solving the problem of consciousness. Maybe our genetically engineered super-mind would see instantly what it is about consciousness that links it to the brain, once the introspective faculty has been given this extended scope. Think of this process as being similar to the invention of the microscope: suddenly a whole new level of reality is opened up and old puzzles begin to fade away. What we are contemplating is a genetically engineered microscope for consciousness, a biological device for seeing right into its concealed infrastructure. Maybe such a brain capacity would never evolve naturally, but genetic engineering opens up all sorts of possibilities for mental augmentation that are virtually un-dreamt-of now. So, for all I know, the mind-body problem *is* soluble by a human mind genetically engineered in the right way.

But here I must issue a stern warning: even if the usual ethical objections to such a project are put on one side, there is the question of what our experimental subject might *lose* as the cost of what he gains. You might naively think that height is a good thing, and so try to produce taller people (I am only 5'6", and don't share this prejudice). But you forget that taller means heavier, which puts more stress on bones. Your race of ten-footers might suffer from early and chronic back problems and other skeletal ailments. As they say, be careful what you wish for! Similarly, the changes in brain structure that might be required to solve the mind-body problem might be so dramatic that the individual would lose much of what makes him human. One of the themes I have harped on is that our predominantly spatial way of representing the world biases us away from understanding consciousness, which is not a spatial phenomenon (at least under our current conception of space). This is no doubt because our bodies are things in space, and their spatial relationship to other things—fires, mates, food—largely determines our fate. But if we need a form of intelligence that does not represent the world in this way, then we might have to give up this basic way of representing things. Maybe the laws of neural circuitry prevent us from having both spatial and nonspatial cognition. And losing our spatial "take" on the world might prove both perilous and unpleasant. How are we supposed to protect our bodies from harm if we have no spatial awareness, all our awareness now being focused on the nonspatial phenomenon of consciousness? And what would it be like to live a life in which we had no such awareness of our body and the outside world? We might have the pleasure of knowing the answer to the mind-body problem, but the rest of life might be bleak and unsatisfying.

It is often said that emotions are an impediment to clear thinking. Does this mean that it is wise to give up having emotions just so that we can think more clearly? True, we would benefit from clearer thoughts, but think of the costs! So it may be that the kind of mind that could solve the mind-body problem is the kind of mind we would rather not have. People often speak enviously of the kind of mind God is supposed to have: omniscient, omnipotent, perfect in every way. But is it really clear that we would *like* to have a mind like God? Much of the pleasure in life comes from learning new things, but God can never experience that pleasure, because he knows everything to begin with. And are we sure that we would want to live a life in which our whims turn effortlessly into reality? Where is the sense of achievement in that? Imagine if the kind of psychology needed to solve the mind-body problem made a person an outcast among human kind, a freak, a monster. That might not be a price he or she would be willing to pay. It is generally good to know things, but not if this means losing other qualities we value more. If someone asked me now whether I wanted to have my brain redesigned in such a way as to give me the solution to the mind-body problem, I would insist on a written guarantee that I would not change in other respects. But I doubt that such a guarantee would be forthcoming. The human mind cannot be tampered with in one area and stay the same elsewhere. We all know this from our experience of the transition from childhood to adulthood: our minds grow and change as the years pass, and we acquire mental faculties we value. But we also lose the joy of innocent childhood. I myself am quite sure that acquiring an ability to "do" philosophy has made me less good at finding my way around the place. Nature being what it is, every silver lining tends to come with its own cloud in tow. It is not clear, then, that cognitive closure with respect to the mind-body problem is something we should bemoan, everything being considered. It depends entirely on what the costs of removing it might be, and about that we can say very little. Even if we could genetically engineer a brain that could solve the problem, it might be a brain no one would want to be stuck with.

## Philosophical Genes

Another question entirely is whether our ignorance is shared by the rest of the universe. Since alien anthropology is in a primitive condition, there not being many aliens around to investigate, we are not in a position to identify any other minds that might have the power to solve the problems that so baffle us. But does that exhaust the range of entities that might be cognitively superior to us in this respect? I want to suggest, perhaps surprisingly, that the *genes* may contain the solution to the mind-body problem. Here I must be careful not to be misunderstood. I am not saying that the genes *know* the solution to the mind-body problem, that they have thought about it and come up with the answer in their little gene minds. Genes do not have minds. They are not conscious. They do not know anything. But this evident fact does not imply that genes cannot contain *information* which is such that, if *we* knew it, we would know the solution. For not all information is carried by conscious mental states. Our visual system, for example, processes information about the environment, although this information is not consciously represented, except for the final product. Information requires basically that there be a symbolic system with semantic properties, and nothing in this description requires that the information be conscious. There is information in a system if there are symbols in it that refer to things and that together form strings that can be true or false. My suggestion then is that the genes contain an informational system in this sense and that this system contains the solution to the mind-body problem.

There are two facets to this argument. The first is that it is indeed appropriate to speak of a genetic symbol system; the second is that there is reason to think that this system contains information about the mind-brain link. In support of the first proposition, let me adduce the fact that this is the way geneticists talk about the genes.[3] They regularly say that the genes contain *instructions* for building bodies of such-and-such a kind. Hence the familiar idea that there is a genetic *code*, a symbolic system that contains information about the kind of organism that will be produced. The DNA uses this code in its construction work: it reads off the instructions written in the code. It works in many ways like a computer, itself an unconscious symbol-manipulating device. Sometimes, unfortunately, these instructions are to build some bodily structure that is bad for the organism; we call that a defective gene, containing misguided instructions. Sometimes the instruction is not carried out correctly because of environmental mishaps. The instructions are like a recipe for building a body, or a program that is to be followed. But notice that all this talk is highly semantic: the process of constructing an organism is driven by symbols with significance, just as visual perception is driven by a subconscious system of symbolic operations. This is precisely why geneticists speak so readily of the "language of the genes." We need not fuss over whether "language" is the right word here; the important point is that genes work by exploiting information about organisms:

*specifications.* They contain a "blueprint" for building an organism, a "manual." They do not cause an organism to exist in the way wind causes trees to bend, by simple mechanical force. Rather, the process is properly explained by reference to informational properties of the genes, what they *represent.* Your genes represent the organism (the "phenotype") you will become.

The genes clearly contain a wealth of biological information. The bodies of animals of different species are vastly different from one another, and their genes must specify a bodily structure that differs from other logically possible bodily structures. The heart is thus shaped, the kidneys are located here, the blood has such-and such-composition, the brain is organized like so. Every detail needs its specific instruction, or else a zebra might have a sheep's heart or just a formless lump where the heart should be. But what goes for the body also goes for the mind: the minds of different species also differ in their "anatomy." The mental organs of cats differ from those of snakes, as ours differ from those of apes. These differences are not learned, as if we could give a cat a snake mind just by raising it as a snake. They are genetically determined, hardwired. So there must be suitable instructions in the genes for engineering this mind or that. There must also be instructions detailing how to build an organism that is *conscious*, because that also is a genetically determined trait of organisms. Animals do not *learn* how to be conscious; consciousness is thrust upon them by their innate biological nature. Consciousness changes and grows as a result of a pre-set genetic program as the organism matures, but the basic plan is fixed by the genes ahead of time.

But now we can note an obvious fact: the genes have to engineer consciousness from matter, from initially insensate biological tissue. The sperm and egg that you came from were not originally conscious at all, yet the genes within them contained the information needed to ensure that you ended up with a conscious mind. They contained instructions for manipulating matter in such a way that consciousness emerged out of it. Not only does DNA cause matter to generate consciousness as the organism grows; it also contains the appropriate *specifications* for generating consciousness. But this means that the genes contain the information that is necessary and sufficient to bring this about. The laws and principles that underlie the connection between mind and brain are somehow encoded into the genes. If we use the metaphor of knowledge, we can say that the genes know how to generate consciousness from matter. They do it all the time, every time they build a new conscious organism. More cautiously and literally, they contain information which is such that if we were to know it we would know the solution to the mind-body problem. In a certain sense, then, the genes are the greatest of philosophers, the repositories of valuable pieces of philosophical information.

Is this surprising? Not really. We have to do many onerous things in our lives, but one of them is not to build an organism from scratch. If we want to create an organism, we do it the easy, fun way: we have sex and reproduce. We hand the job of actually constructing the full-blown organism over to our DNA, which is much better at it than we are. Sperm and egg join, the DNA gets to work, and in a matter of weeks we have a recognizable human embryo, and eventually a towering adult. That is the job nature has assigned to the genes: to manufacture whole functioning organisms from slender beginnings. But it is not, thank goodness, our job. If evolution had equipped us with the intelligence and biological know-how to manufacture organisms, instead of leaving this task to our genes, then it would have made us very differently. But what evolution does is work on a two-level principle: give animals enough intelligence to mate and reproduce, and then let the really fancy stuff be taken care of by their DNA. There is thus no *need* to make us smart enough to create organisms from scratch, while the genes had *better* be able to do it (someone has to). In other words, our minds don't need to contain the information necessary to build a conscious organism because our genes already contain it. So it is not very surprising that the genes contain reserves of information not available to us. Since every cell in your body contains a full copy of your genetic blueprint, a vast library of biological information, we can say that every such cell contains more information about the mind-body relation than your mind ever will (granted the cognitive closure thesis). The mind-body problem is a mystery for your mind but not for your genes.

So, I ask you: how does it feel to be less intelligent than your big toe? (I use the word "intelligent" loosely, but you see my point.)

## How Funny Are We?

I want to end by pondering how *funny* (that is, strange) we are. We are a mysterious amalgam of mind and matter, as are other conscious organisms. We are neither one thing nor the other. A rock is just a rock, a hunk of insentient material; it suffers from no split in its nature. An angel, if there were one, would be pure spirit, not subject to the laws of matter; it too would be a unified being. But we are divided beings, centers of consciousness in a skin-sack of soft tissue. From the point of view of an angel, or a disembodied alien from outer space, we might seem like rather comical beings, peculiar ontological hybrids. Like those mythical beasts combining one animal with another, we are anomalous juxtapositions. It can sometimes seem amazing that I depend for my existence and well-being on my body at all. At other times my body seems to be all I am. It would be so much *simpler* to be either pure matter or pure mind.

The aliens quoted in chapter 1 were bemused by the idea that there could be meat-headed thinking beings; that seemed *truly* alien to them. Meat and mind seemed to them like polar opposites. As far as they were concerned, organically based consciousness is an oxymoron, and a rather disgusting one at that. Maybe their bemusement would descend to crude amusement if they were to capture some of us and put us in cages for their kids to ogle. "Come and look at the meat heads! Conscious beings with spam in their skulls! Genuine alien freaks! Look, they really walk and talk! But please, no feeding the meat-based aliens, our food will only make them ill." They might shake with supersonic laughter at such a peculiar sight. And it can seem pretty funny, in a dark sort of way, when you think about that clump of clammy gray cells in your head that is so indispensable for everything about yourself that you most value. Most of us prefer to pass this thought by; don't go there, please! There is something bizarre and unsettling about what we objectively are.

But maybe we are not as funny as we seem. Maybe we are only superficially freakish. The split in our nature may be more apparent than real. Those laughing aliens are misled, after all. Because, as I have been at pains to argue, in reality something *unifies* mind and body, makes them one. My whole point has been that mind and brain form an indissoluble unity *at the level of objective reality*. In some way we don't understand, consciousness and the brain are intelligible aspects of the same thing, not the chalk and cheese they seem to be. The brain is not just meat and the mind is more than its surface appearance. There is an order underlying the heterogeneous appearances. There has to be, or we would not be possible. Nature abhors a miracle. Objectively, we are naturally constituted from smoothly meshing materials, as seamless as anything else in nature. We only *seem* comical because we cannot grasp what this unified reality consists of. The proper response to the cruelly amused aliens is that we only appear so strange to them because they are ignorant of our true nature. And that is the kind of response that has been called for on numerous occasions in our own history. If we are ever discriminated against by laser-brained aliens because of our meatiness, we can point out that we are really no more peculiar than they are, once the facts are known. Our oddity lies in the eye of the beholder, not in our intrinsic nature. Deep down we are quite ordinary, difficult as that may be to believe.

# Notes

Because the chapters of this book are largely based on other—more technical—writings of mine, there are an embarrassingly large number of references to my own work in the following list of suggested readings, unavoidably so. The main point of the sources is to provide a starting point for further investigation, not an exhaustive and impartial list of what has been written on the topics treated in the book.

## CHAPTER 1

1 Descartes' classic formulation of the certainty of self-knowledge is found in his *Meditations on First Philosophy*, published in 1641. In *The Philosophical Writings of Descartes*, vol. II (Cambridge: Cambridge University Press, 1984).

2 I discuss the themes of this book further in *The Character of Mind* (Oxford: Oxford University Press, 1997), *The Problem of Consciousness* (Oxford: Basil Blackwell, 1991), *Problems in Philosophy* (Oxford: Basil Blackwell, 1993), and *Minds and Bodies* (New York: Oxford University Press, 1997).

3 Terry Bisson's story first appeared on the Internet; it is quoted here from Steven Pinker, *How the Mind Works* (New York: Norton, 1997).

4   For a discussion of black holes and cosmology, see Stephen Hawking, *A Brief History of Time* (New York: Bantam, 1988).

5   This by now famous sentence originally appeared in 1886 in Thomas Huxley's *Elements of Physiology* (London: MacMillan).

6   For a recent attempt to defend materialism, see Daniel Dennett, *Consciousness Explained* (Boston: Little, Brown, 1991).

7   Frank Jackson's argument can be found in his chapter, "What Mary Didn't Know," in D. Rosenthal, ed., *The Nature of Mind* (Oxford: Oxford University Press, 1991).

8   Brian Farrell's original discussion of bats and consciousness appears in his article, "Experience," *Mind,* vol. 59 (1950). Thomas Nagel's much better known discussion appears in the chapter, "What Is It Like to Be a Bat?" in *Mortal Questions* (Cambridge: Cambridge University Press, 1979).

9   For a recent defense of dualism, see David Chalmers, *The Conscious Mind* (New York: Oxford University Press, 1996).

## CHAPTER 2

1   For a discussion of skepticism, see Bertrand Russell, *The Problems of Philosophy* (Oxford: Oxford University Press, 1968; first published 1912).

2   The conception of human intelligence as modular and innate is defended in Noam Chomsky, *Reflections on Language* (New York: Pantheon, 1995) and *Language and Problems of Knowledge* (Cambridge, Mass.: MIT Press, 1988). A recent lengthy defense of this concept appears in Steven Pinker, *How the Mind Works* (New York: Norton, 1997).

3   David Hume's classic work is *A Treatise on Human Nature*, published in 1739. I discuss Humean minds and their limits in "Can We Solve the Mind-Body Problem?" in *The Problem of Consciousness* (Oxford: Basil Blackwell, 1991).

4   I discuss the idea of combination and its role in our thinking in *Problems in Philosophy* (Oxford: Basil Blackwell, 1993).

## CHAPTER 3

1   Richard Dawkins's *The Blind Watchmaker* (New York: Norton, 1986) is an excellent discussion of the argument from design and the Darwinian response to it.

2   Hyperdualism is described and evaluated in my chapter, "Consciousness and Cosmology," in M. Davies and G. Humphreys, eds., *Consciousness: Psychological and Philosophical Essays* (Oxford: Basil Blackwell, 1993).

3   Panpsychism is sympathetically discussed in David Chalmers, *The Conscious Mind* (New York: Oxford University Press, 1996).

## CHAPTER 4

1   My original discussion of the topic of this chapter is in "Consciousness and Space, *The Journal of Consciousness Studies* 2, no. 3 (1995).

2   On the origin of the physical universe, see Stephen Hawking, *A Brief History of Time* (New York: Bantam, 1988).

3   Edwin Abbott's *Flatland* first appeared in 1884. (My edition, New York: Penguin, 1984).

## CHAPTER 5

1   I first wrote about the topic of this chapter in "The Hidden Structure of Consciousness," in *The Problem of Consciousness* (Oxford: Basil Blackwell, 1991).

2   Bertrand Russell's theory of descriptions is set out in his *Introduction to Mathematical Philosophy* (London: George Allen & Unwin, 1919), written while he was in prison during the First World War.

3   For the empirical facts of blindsight, see Lawrence Weiskrantz, *Blindsight: A Case-Study and Implications* (Oxford: Oxford University Press, 1986).

4   For a discussion of personal identity, see my books *The Charac-*
    *ter of Mind* (Oxford: Oxford University Press, 1997) and *Prob-*
    *lems in Philosophy* (Oxford: Basil Blackwell, 1993).
5   For a philosophical treatment of split-brain cases, see Thomas
    Nagel, "Brain Bisection and the Unity of Consciousness," in
    *Mortal Questions* (Cambridge: Cambridge University Press,
    1979). See also Michael Gazzaniga and J. E. De Loux, *The Inte-*
    *grated Mind* (New York: Plenum Press, 1978).
6   Such a view of the self is endorsed by Daniel Dennett in *Con-*
    *sciousness Explained* (Boston: Little, Brown, 1991).
7   I discuss free will more fully in *Problems in Philosophy* (Oxford:
    Basil Blackwell, 1993).

## CHAPTER 6

1   John Searle criticizes the computer model of the mind in *Minds,*
    *Brains and Science* (Cambridge, Mass.: Harvard University
    Press, 1984). I also criticize it in *The Character of Mind* (Oxford:
    Oxford University Press, 1997).
2   The Turing test made its first appearance in Alan Turing, "Com-
    puting Machinery and Intelligence," *Mind,* vol. 59 (1950).
3   I discuss the different meanings of "machine" in "Could a Ma-
    chine be Conscious?," in *The Problem of Consciousness* (Oxford:
    Basil Blackwell, 1991).

## CHAPTER 7

1   The interpretation of the history of thought put forward in this
    chapter can also be found in my book *Problems in Philosophy*
    (Oxford: Basil Blackwell, 1993).
2   For a survey of the history of thought, see Bertrand Russell, *His-*
    *tory of Western Philosophy* (London: George Allen & Unwin, 1946).
3   Richard Dawkins works with a strongly symbolic conception of
    DNA in his *The Blind Watchmaker* (New York: Norton, 1986).

# Index